Beefcake Buffet

A NAKEDCOMIX ADULT COLORING BOOK

BY JAMES COURTNEY

I0482862

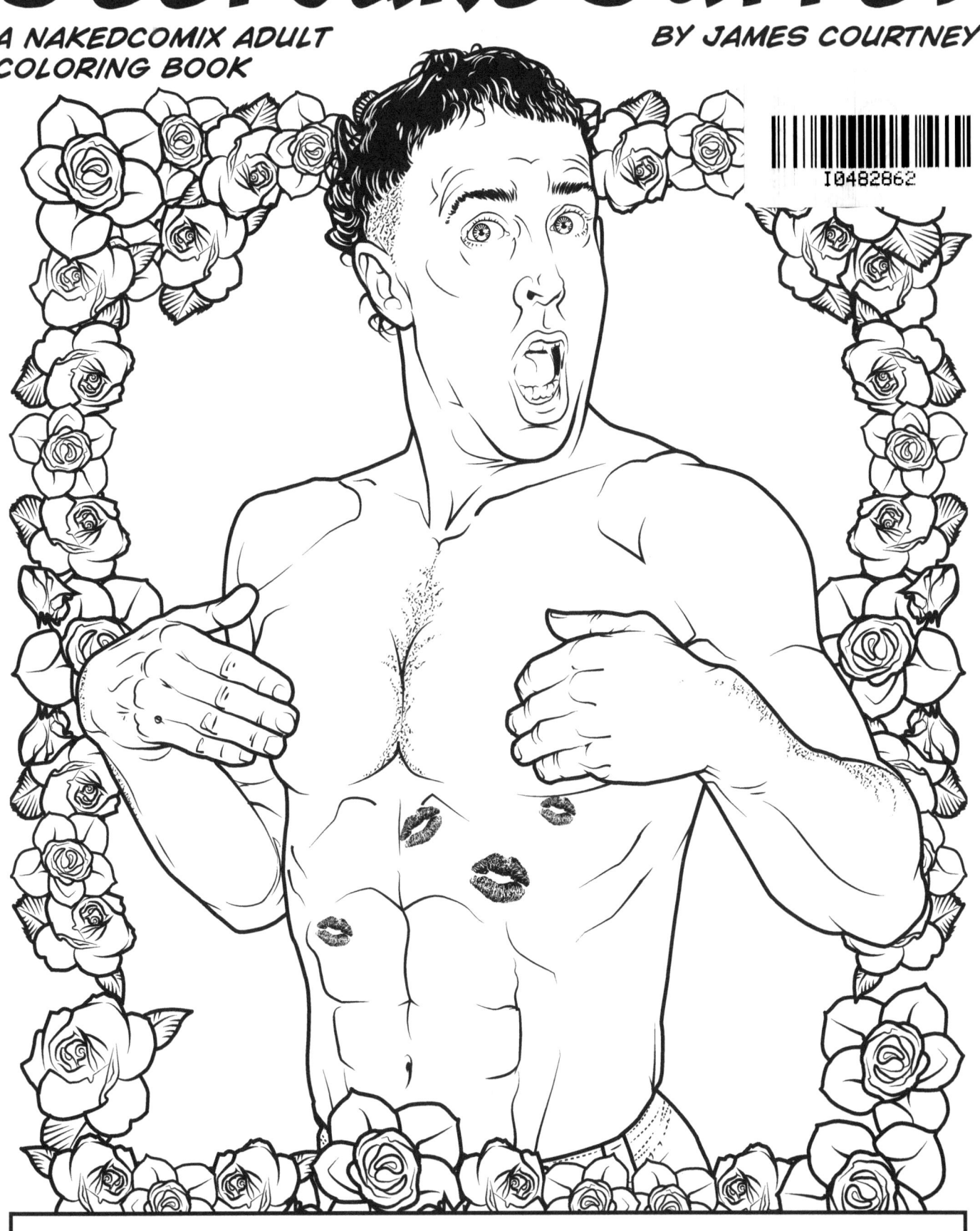

FOLLOW US ON
FACEBOOK & IG

BOOK
TWO

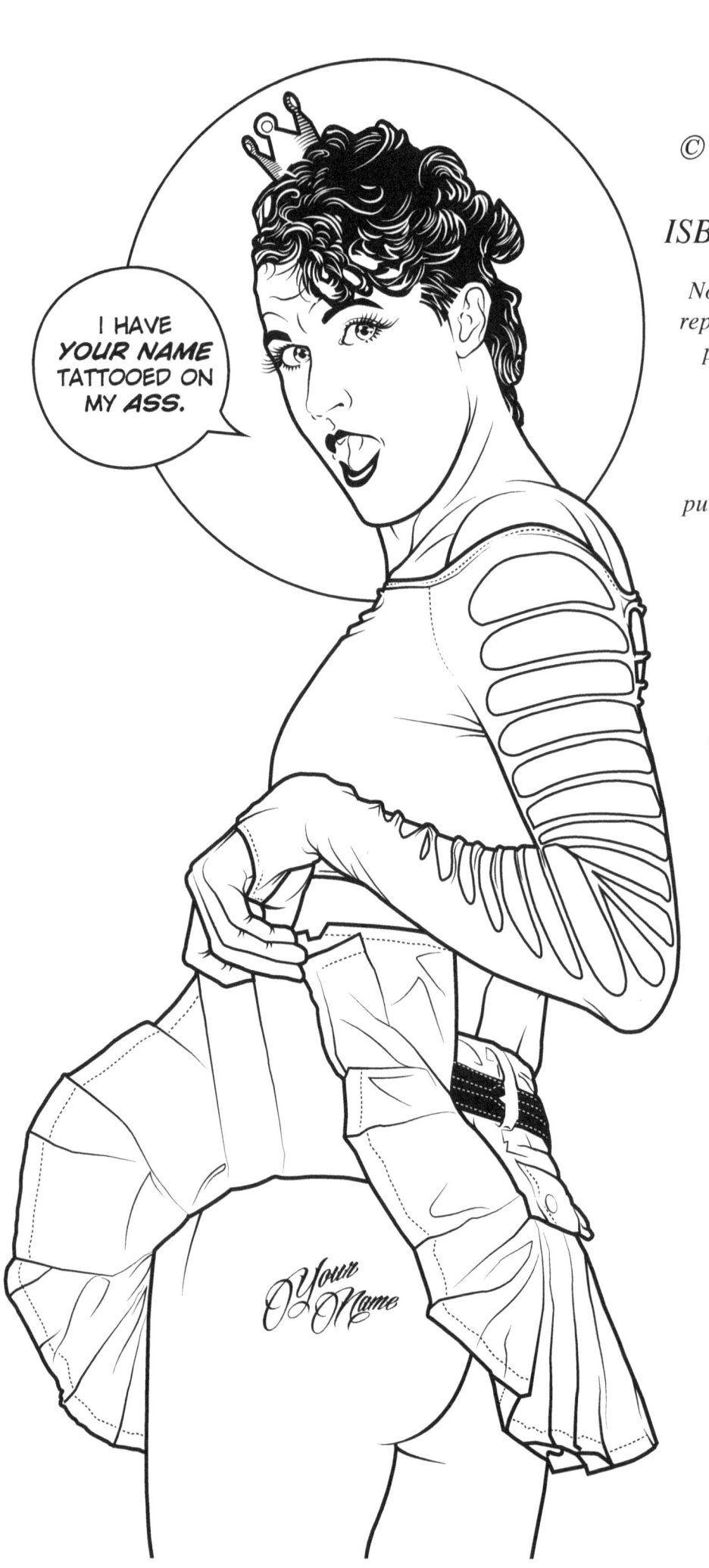

Nakedcomix #2:
Beefcake Buffet

© 2022 James Courtney
All rights reserved.
ISBN 978-0-9858999-6-7

**Dedicated to
all the models who
posed for this, and
all my other coloring
books. I couldn't do
this without you all.
Thanks**

When I first started doing coloring books, I filled them with images that I felt comfortable with and enjoyed drawing, which were women. Later, when I worked on the Burlesque Coloring Book and Nakedcomix #1, I added some male burlesque performers to the mix. However, when I decided to start work on this book, I knew I had to change the type of model I was offering my audience. Most coloring book buyers are women, and the one thing they consistently ask to see are more images of men. So, I decided to make this book completely about male models.

As a straight, male, artist, this involved some changes to my thinking. Art in general is geared for the male gaze, but I wanted to make art shaped for the female gaze. As author Rita Mae Brown once advised, I needed to work on a sort of "intellectual bi-sexuality". I never really thought about what women found sexy about men. I couldn't just come at this from the standard cisgender male viewpoint. It took me a long

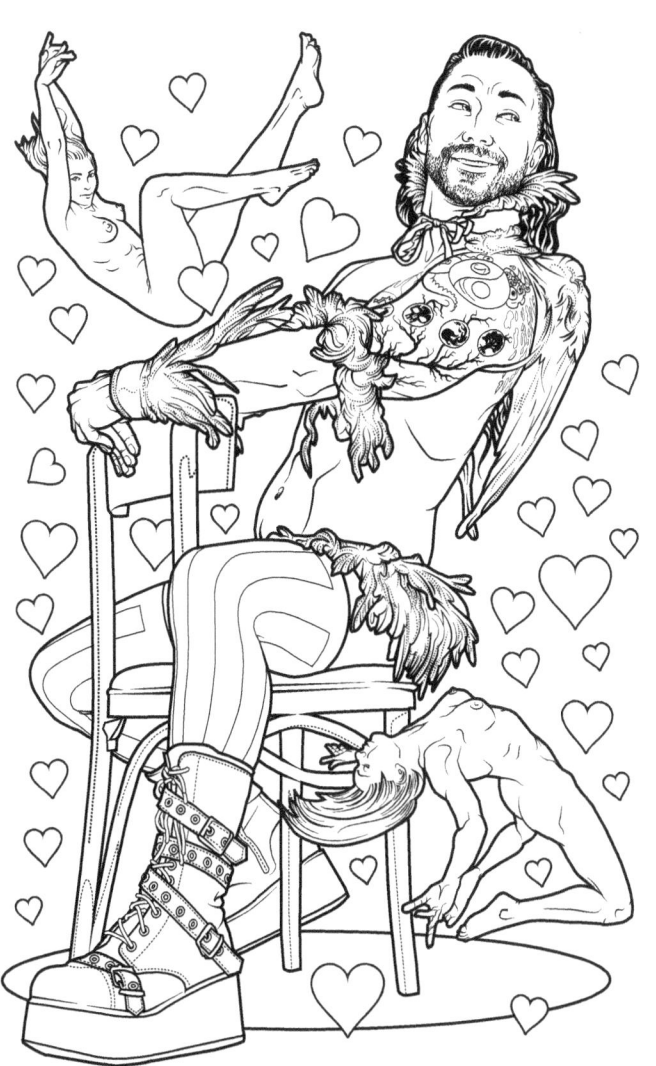

conversation with a bisexual male friend to figure out what people "check-out" in men compared to what they "check-out" in women.

It was hard to work on a project like this. It drove home how often I was thinking in terms of gender roles and not realizing it, just thinking on autopilot. At least two of the female models I included in my earlier Kinky Coloring Books have transitioned to men. If I shot with them today, I would do so with an entirely different viewpoint. The trick to understanding diversity was first embracing the depth of my own ignorance.

Finding male models to work with was the second challenge. Shooting exclusively male models was a growth experience for me. I couldn't just let "tits, ass, and a pretty face" carry things (and I realize how often I had previously done just that.). I had to work on more of my photographer skills to get a sexy image. Things like posing, lighting, and specifically directing became more important in my mind. Many of my male models didn't know how to be "sexy" like my female models did. It took a bit of exploration and work to get that groove going. In the end, many of the lessons I learned from working with female models translated over to male models without change: create a safe space to be in, communicate, collaborate, get comfortable, and have fun. The last two are very important. It is universally impossible to look sexy if you are uncomfortable and not having fun with it.

Though I learned a lot making it, the purpose of this coloring book is for you to have fun. I hope you enjoy coloring all the sexy guys in here. It has been an honor and a privilege creating it for you. Color away.

James Courtney

Cover Model: Guy Vigor
Front Page Model: Ross Travis
Left Model: Wonder Dave
Right Model: Leon G. Ray

Woodland Elf

Model: Proteus Waterflame

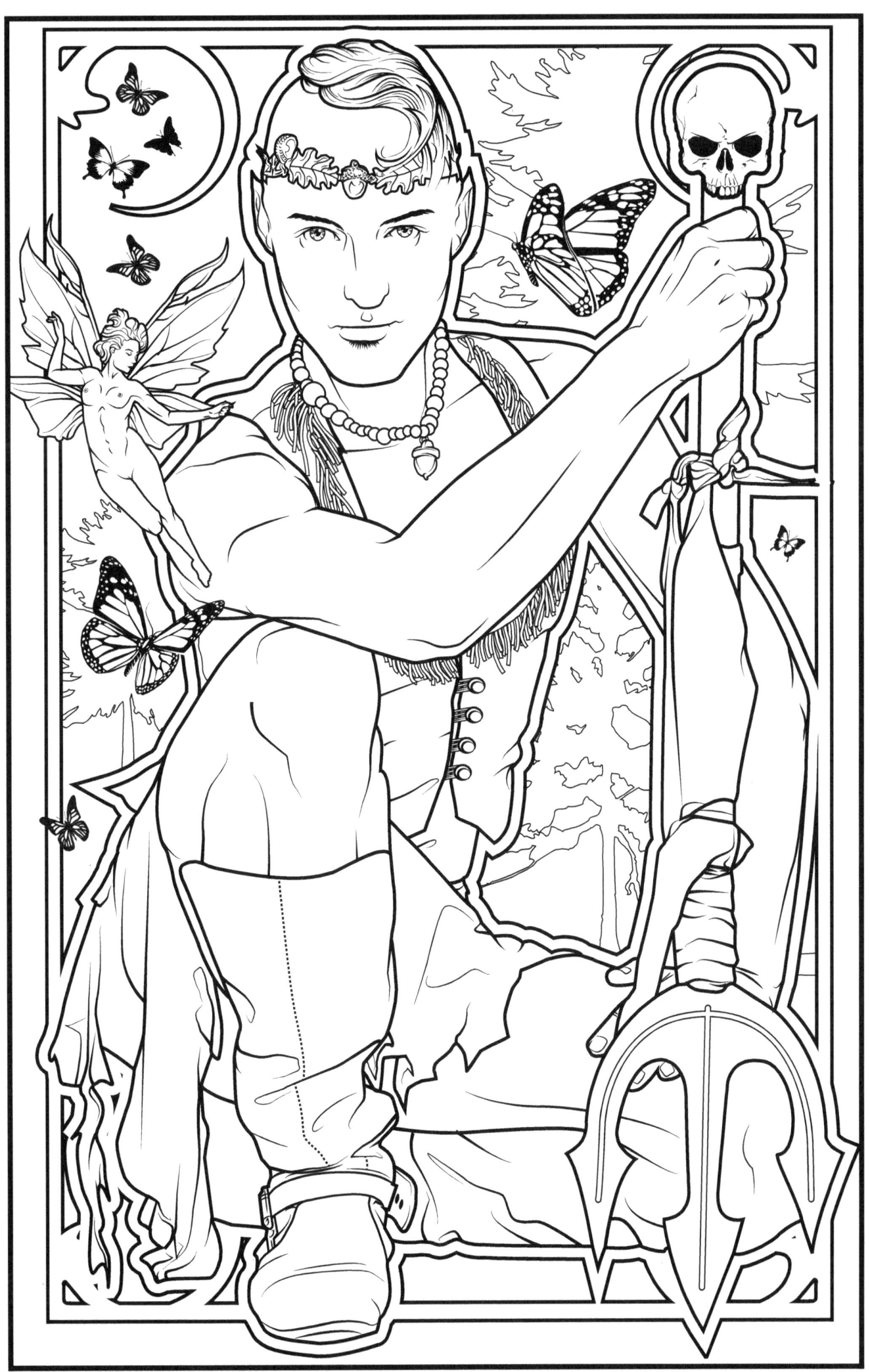

Alien-Abduction

Model: Sugar Buns

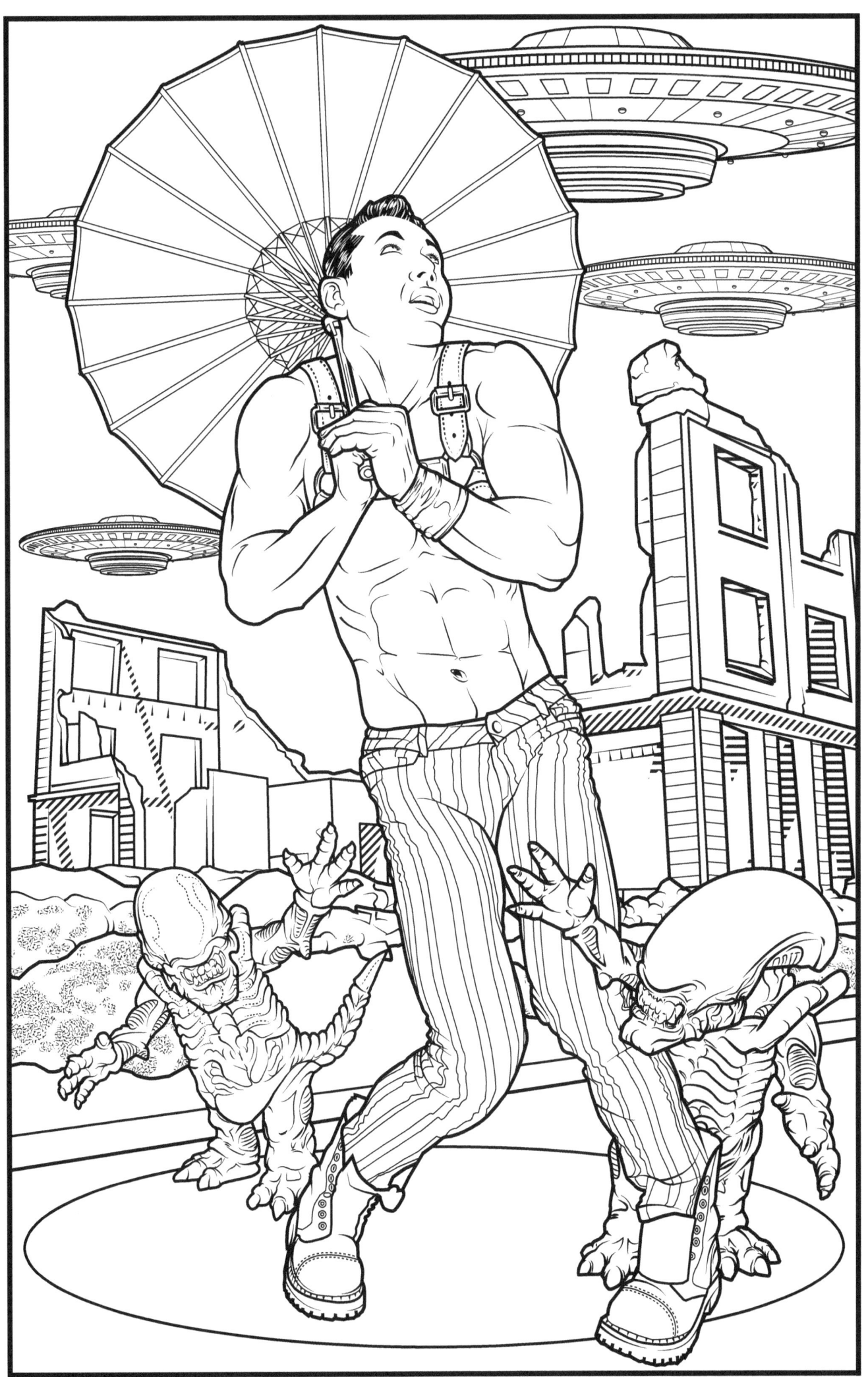

Closer look

Model: Twitch

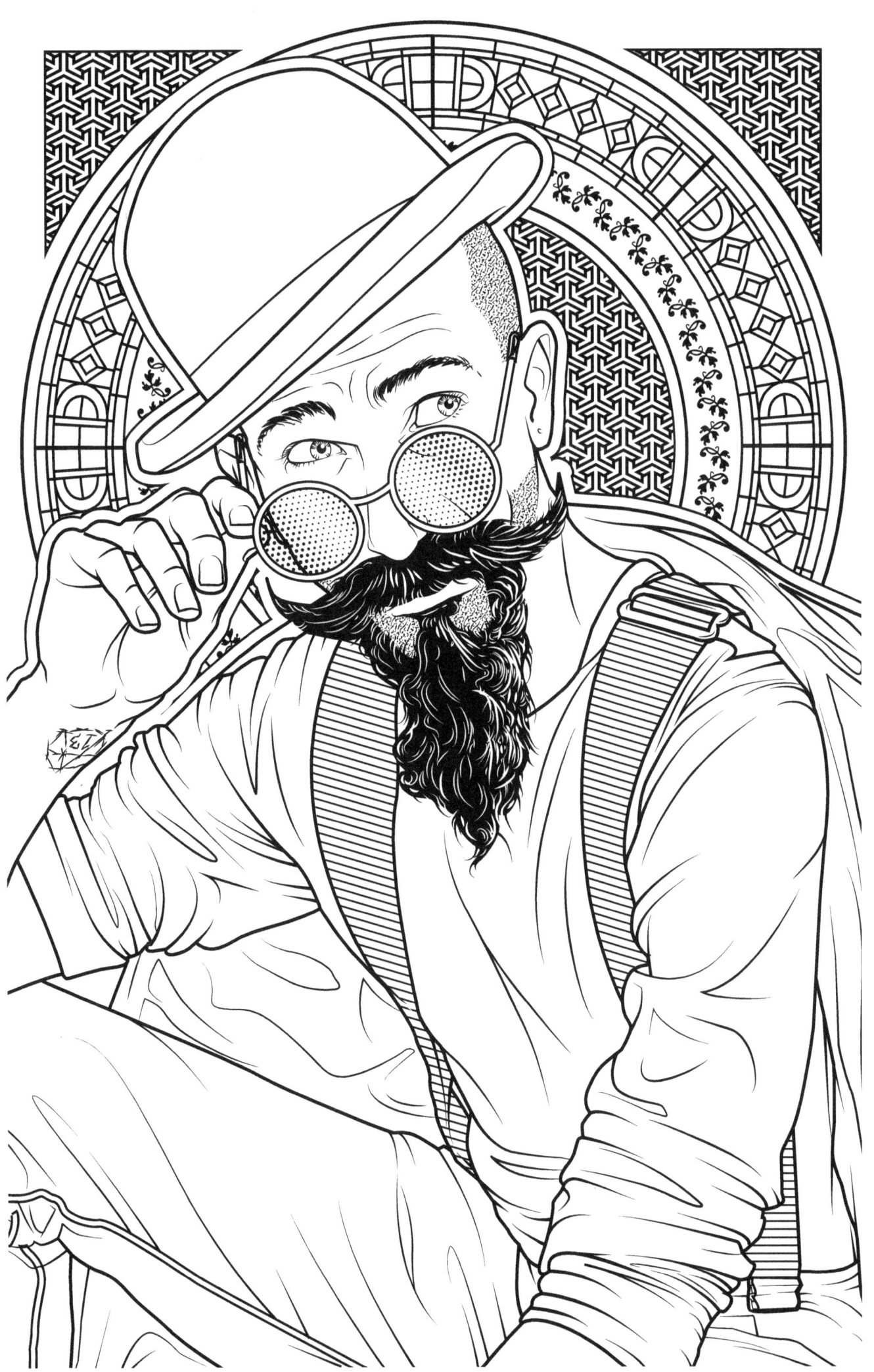

Santa's Dilemma

Model: Jet Noir

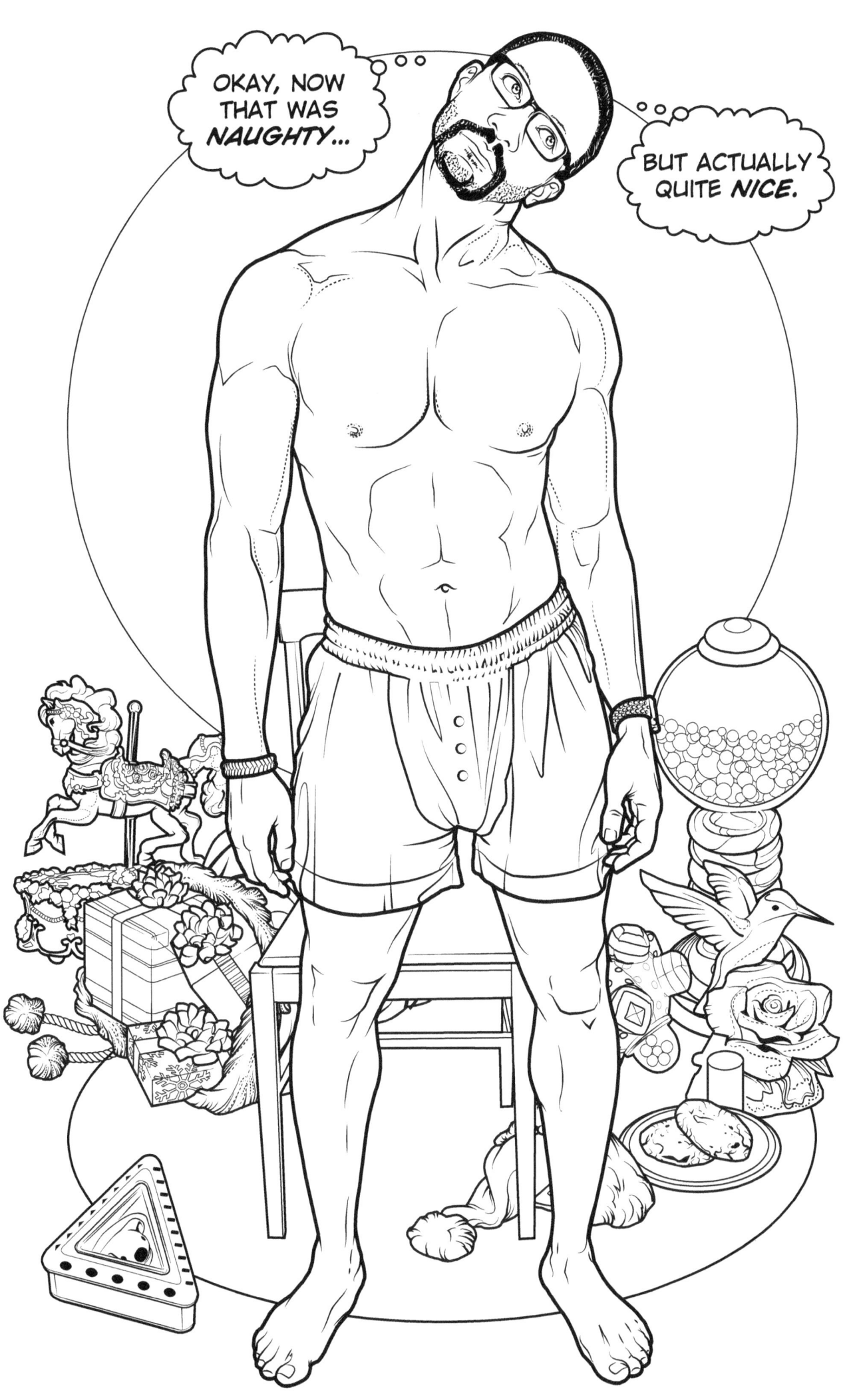

Making Hats

Model: Trevor

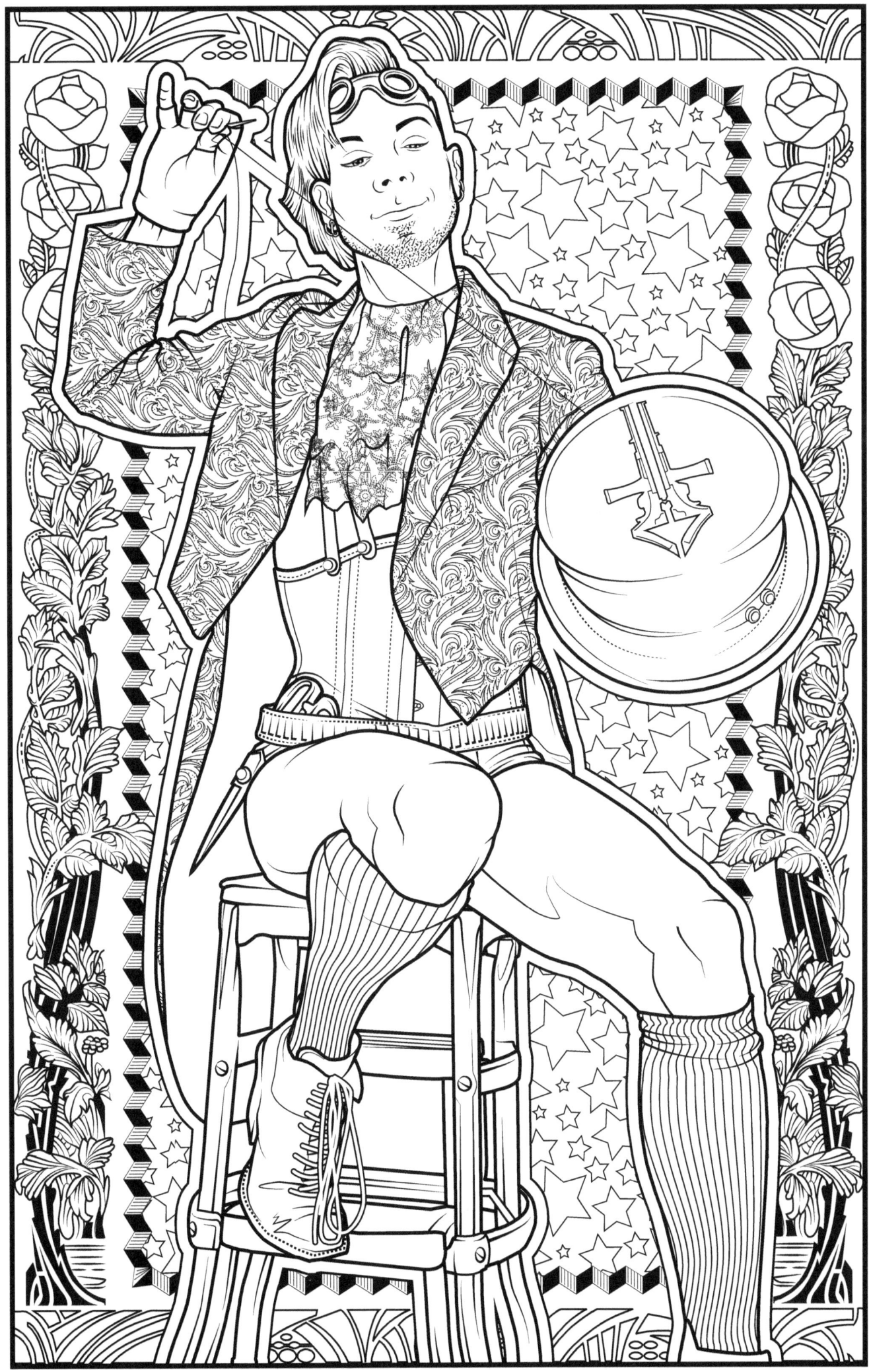

The Painter

Model: Lee Harvey Roswell

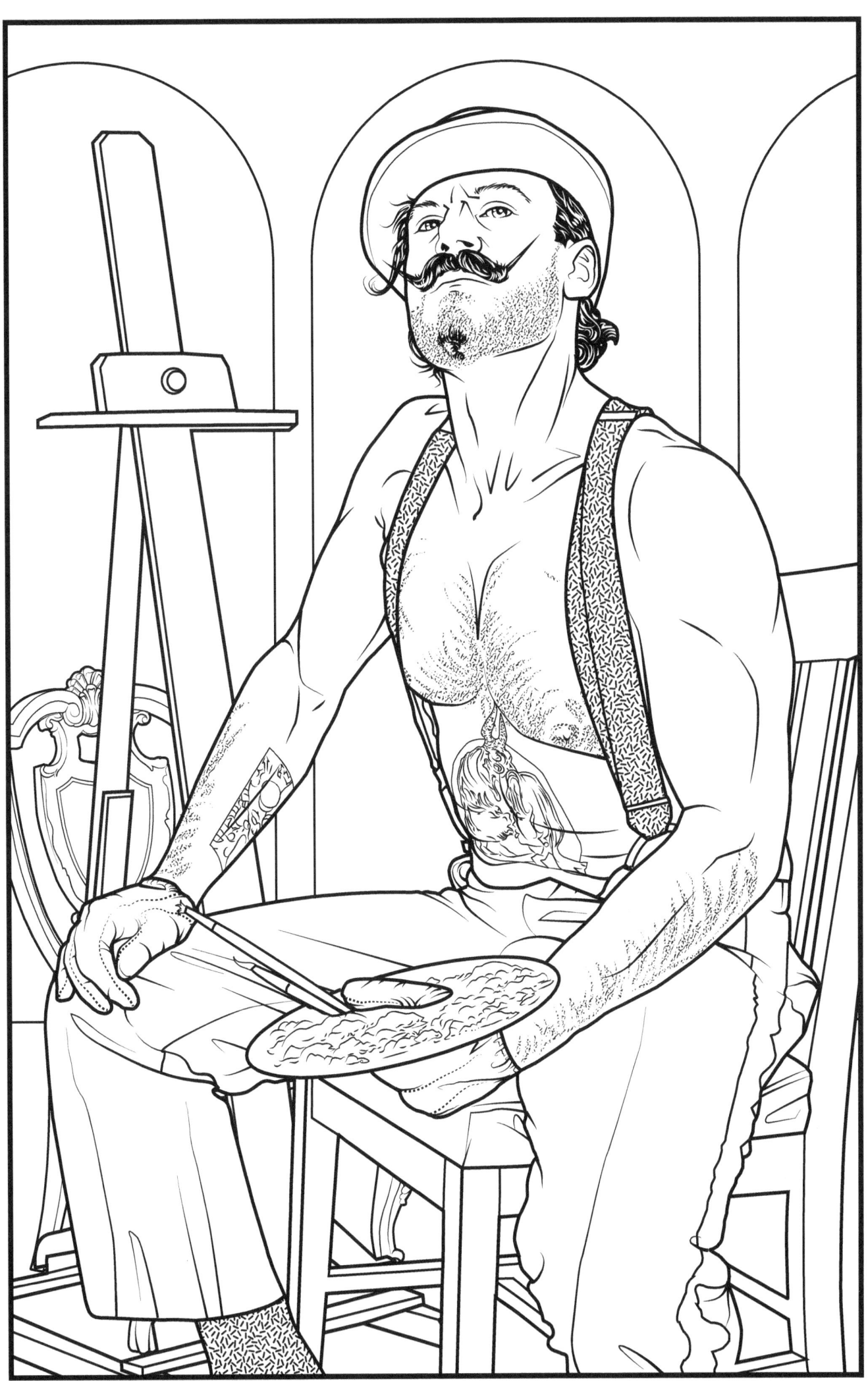

Among The Stars

Model: Aaron of Little Boxes Theater

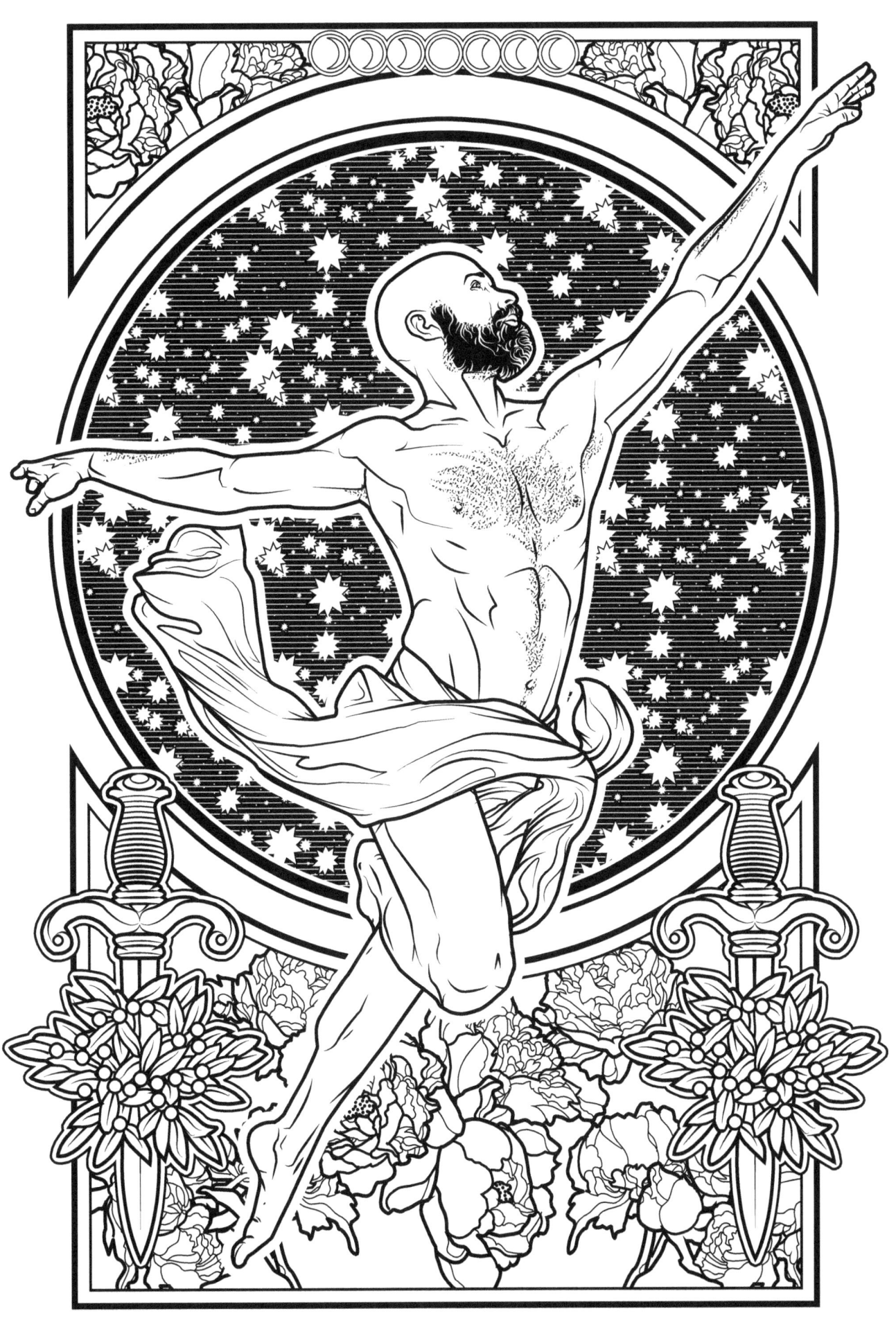

Cowboy Portrait

Model: Proteus Waterflame

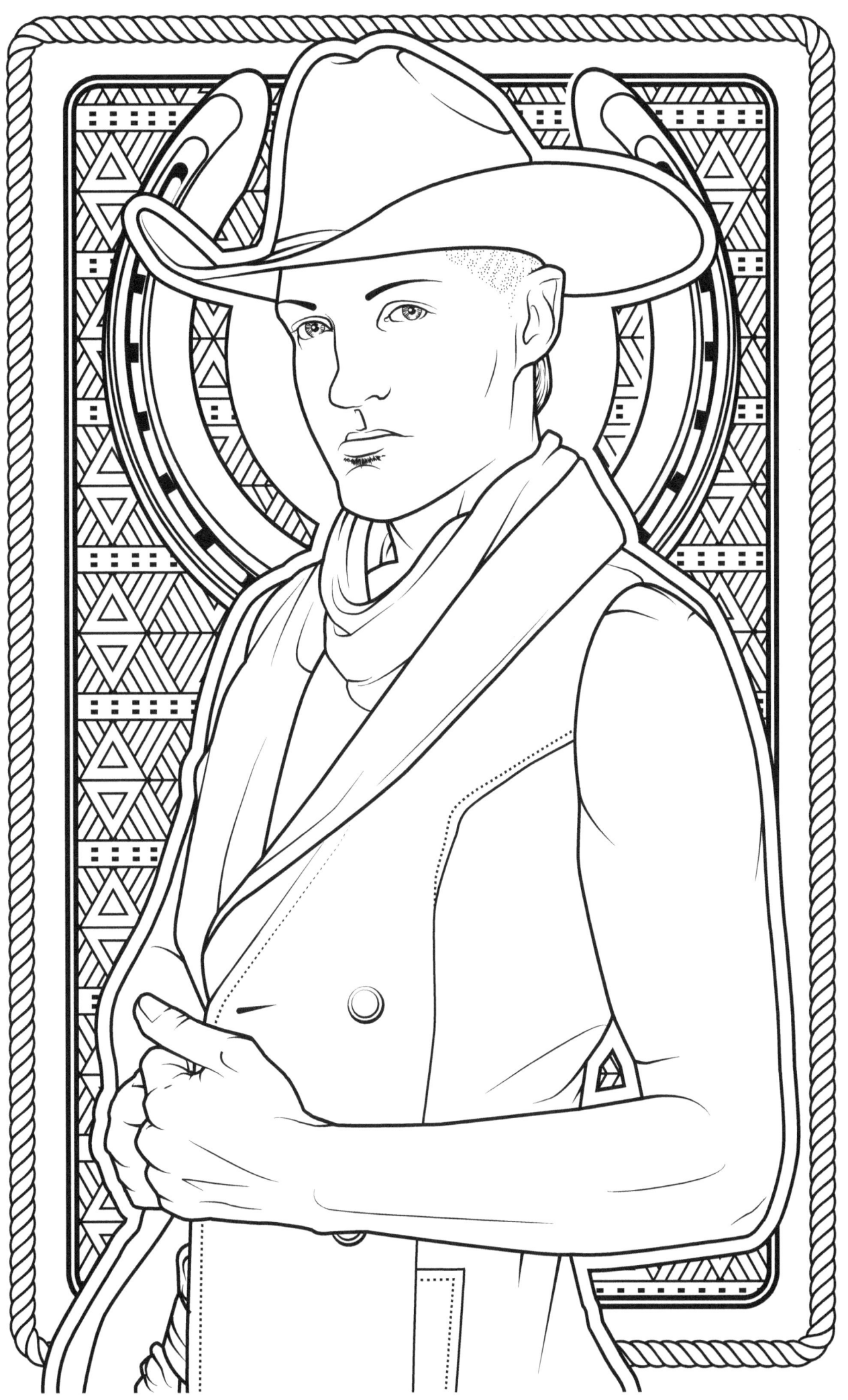

Happiness Is...

Model: Dani Red and The Facilitator

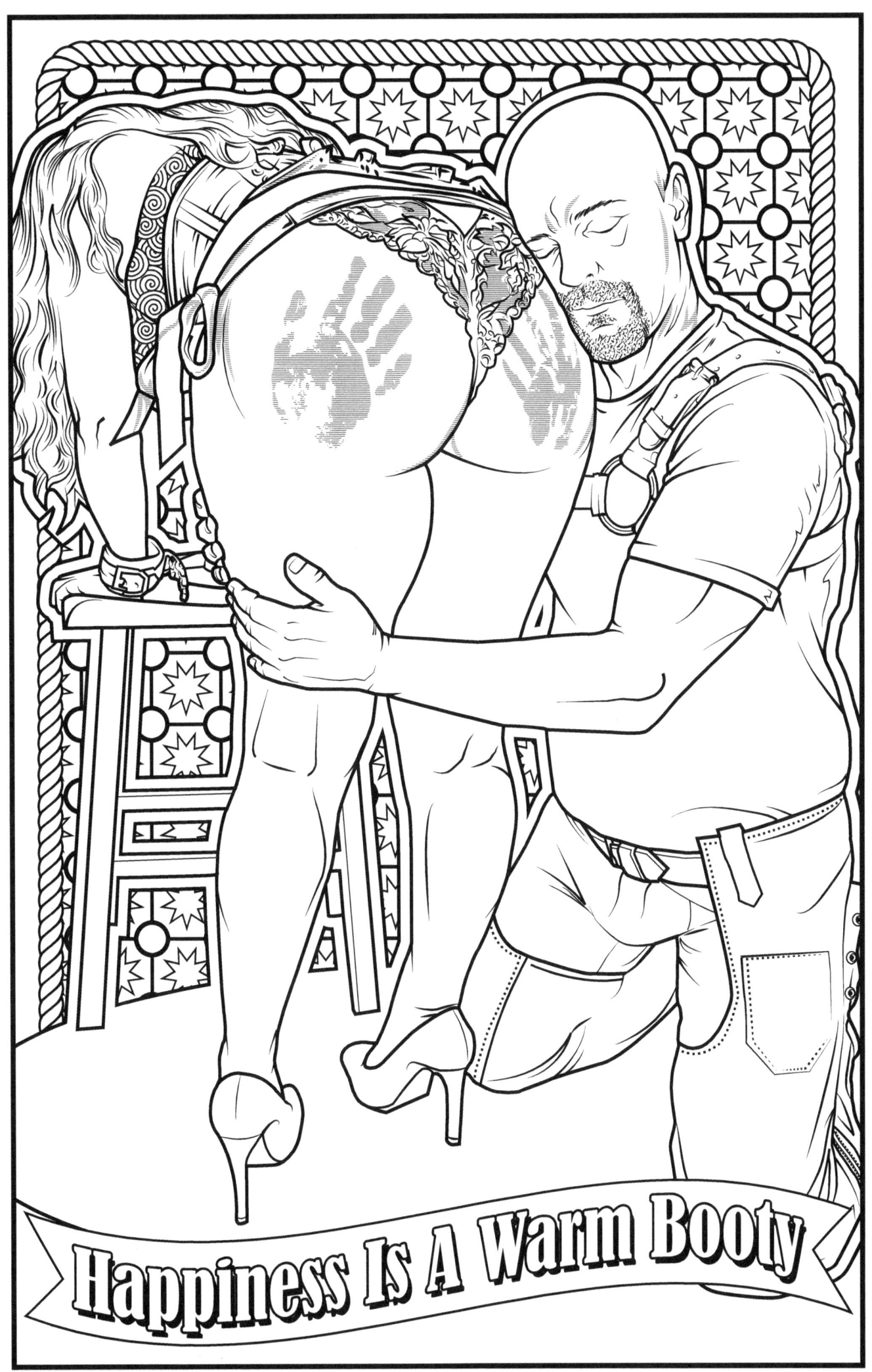

Happiness Is A Warm Booty

The Major

Model: Major Suttle-Tease

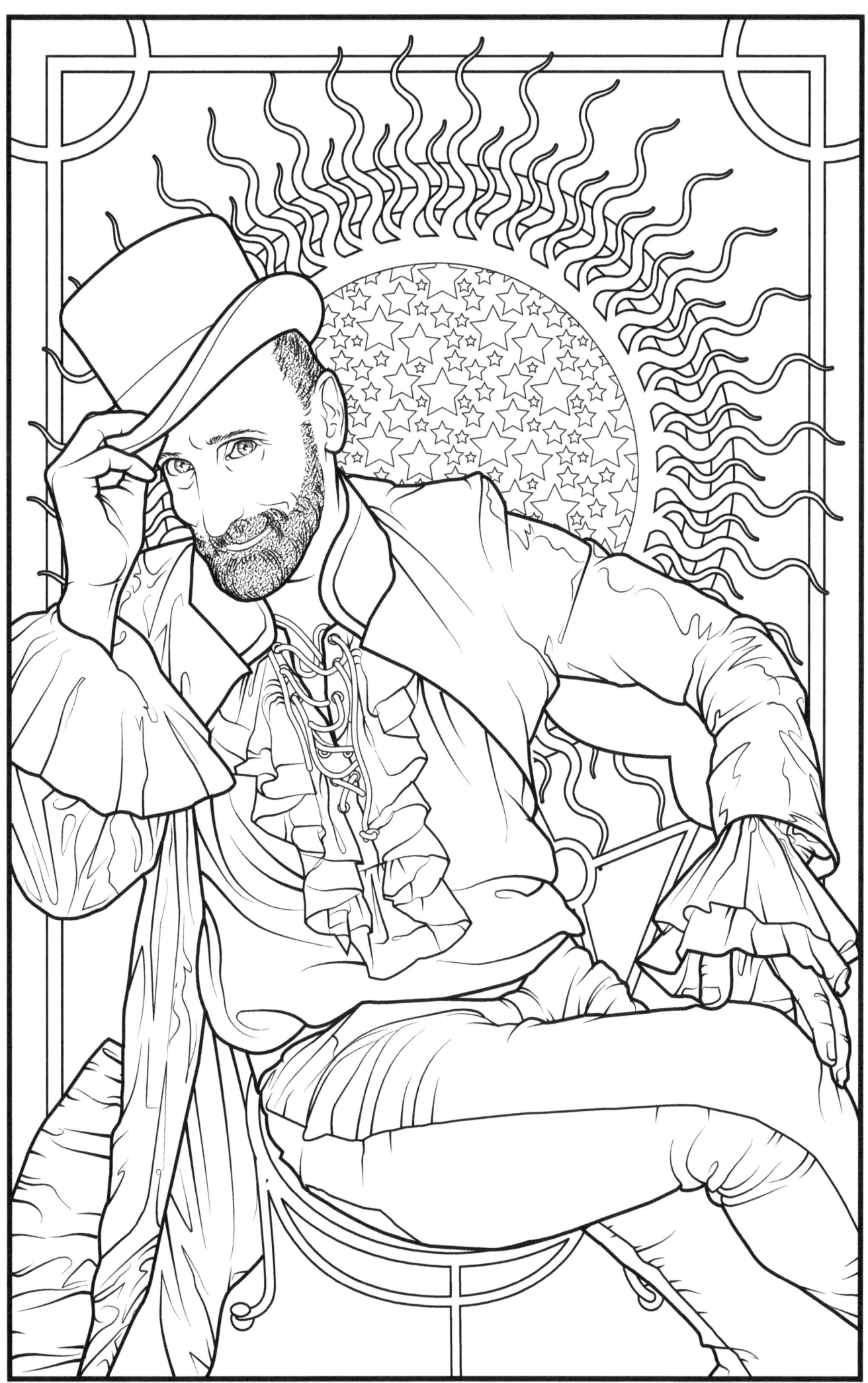

Balance

Model: Seanmichael Polaris

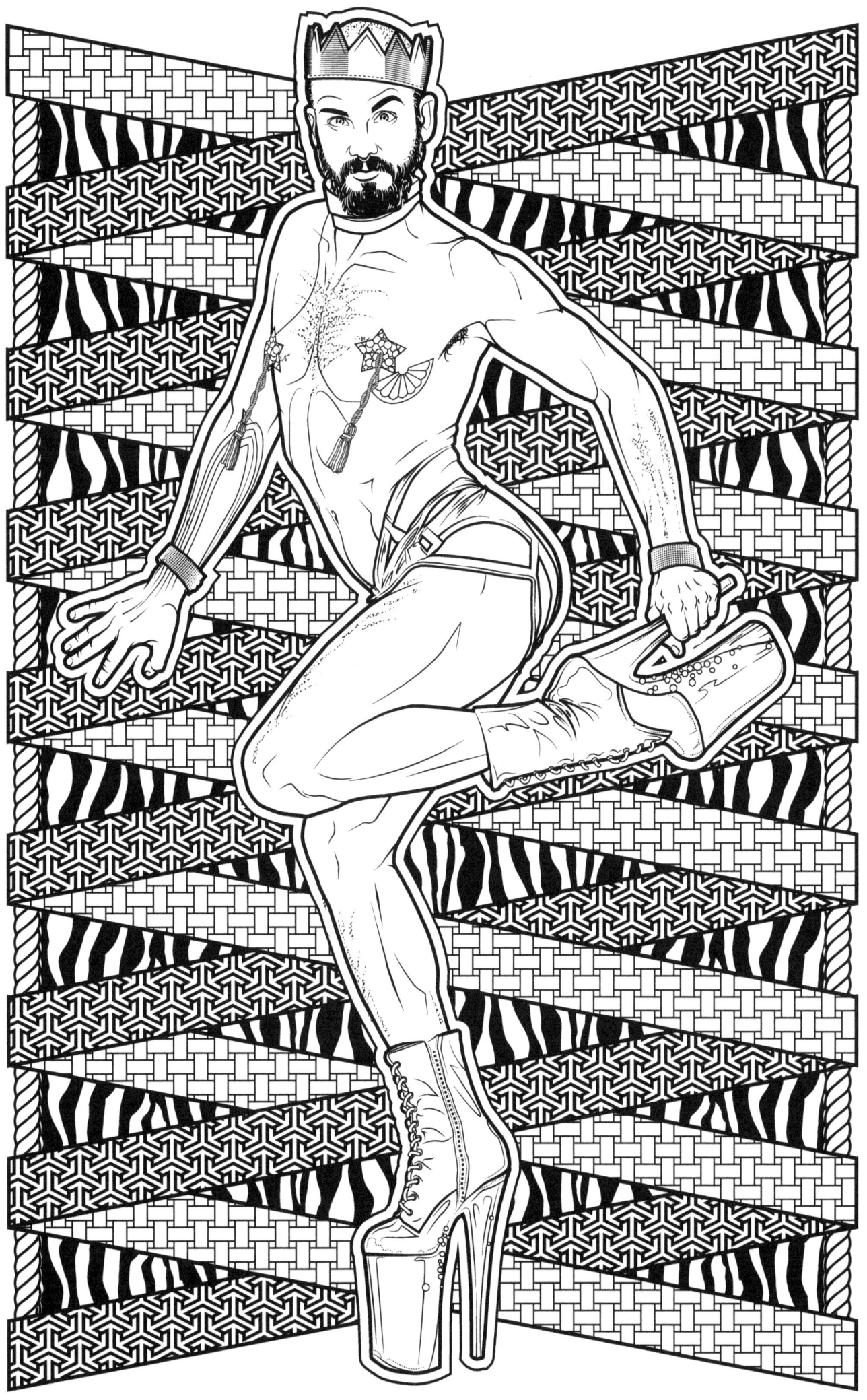

Bartender

Model: Benjamin Carter Jr.

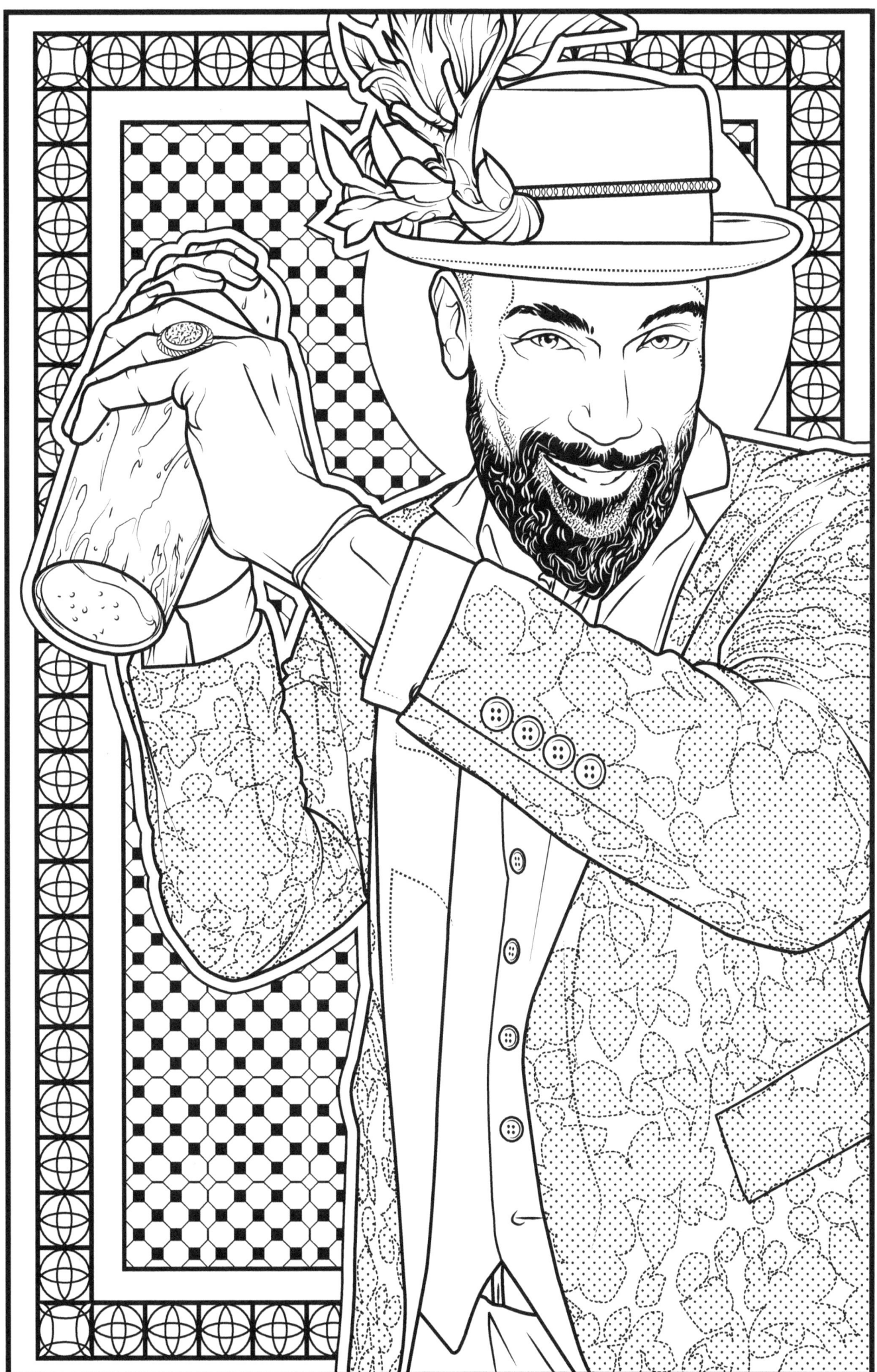

The Rocker

Model: Ken Newman

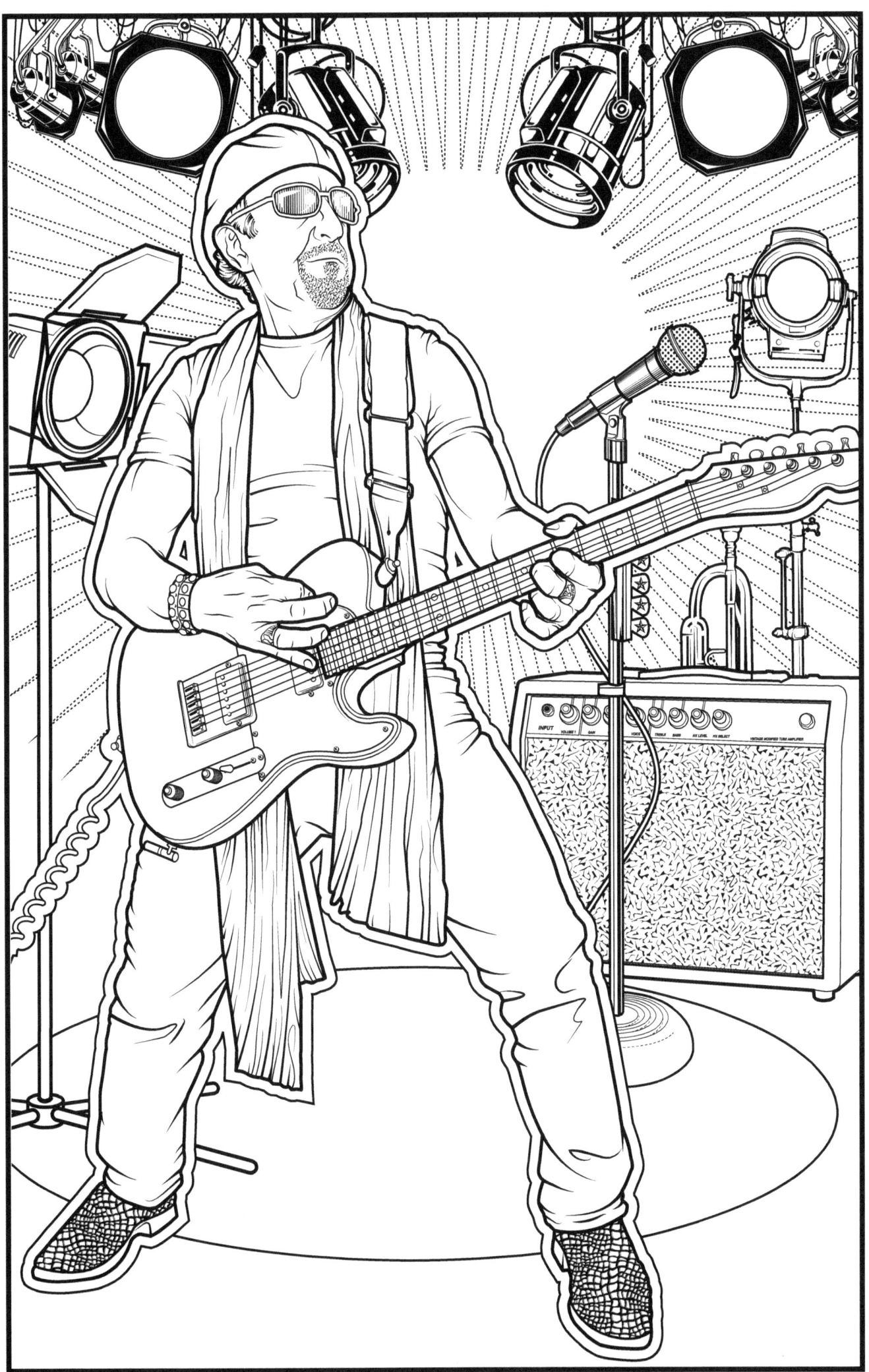

Daddy's Home

Model: Matthew James

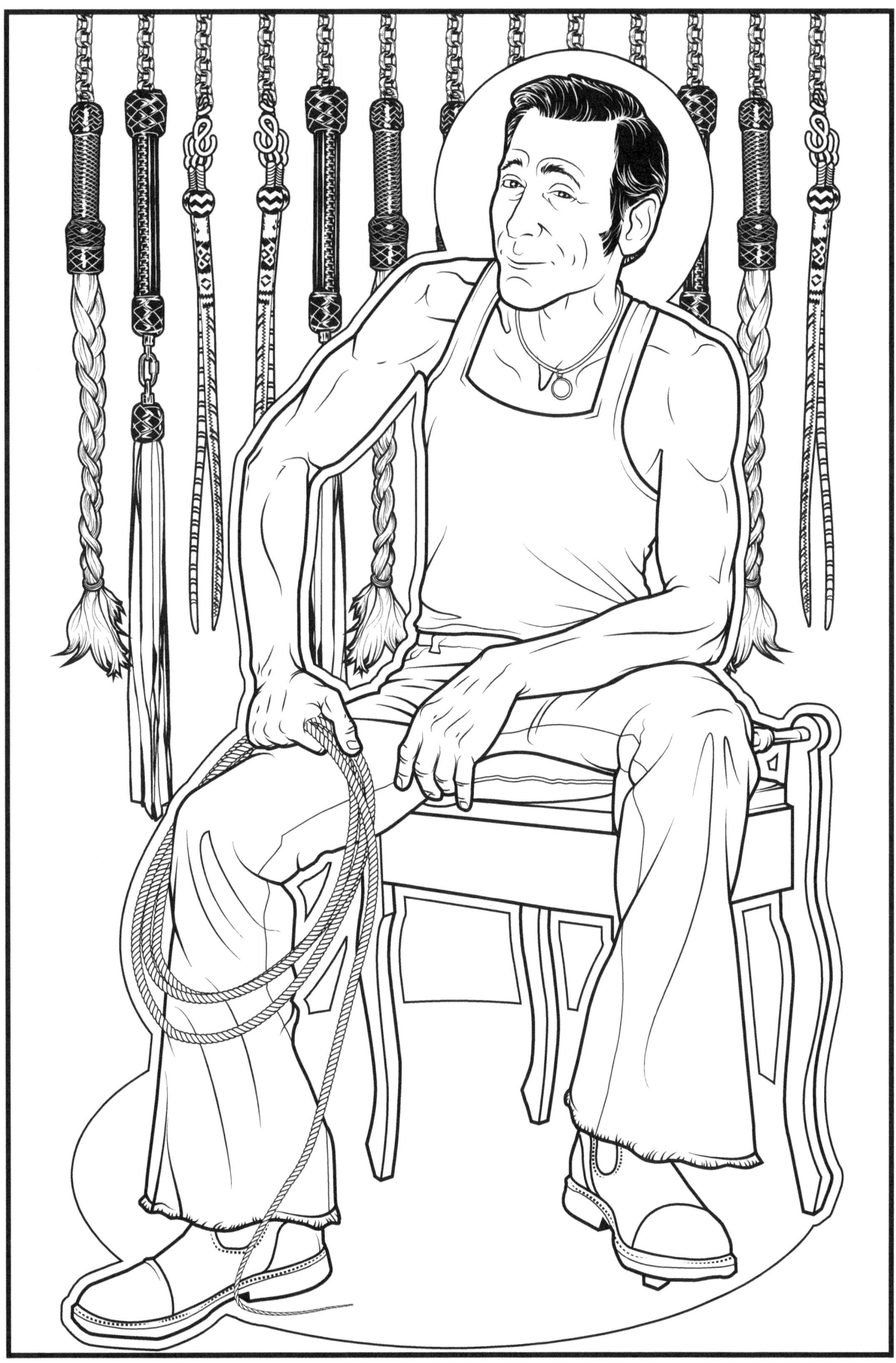

The Irish Bouncer

Model: Benjamine Wester

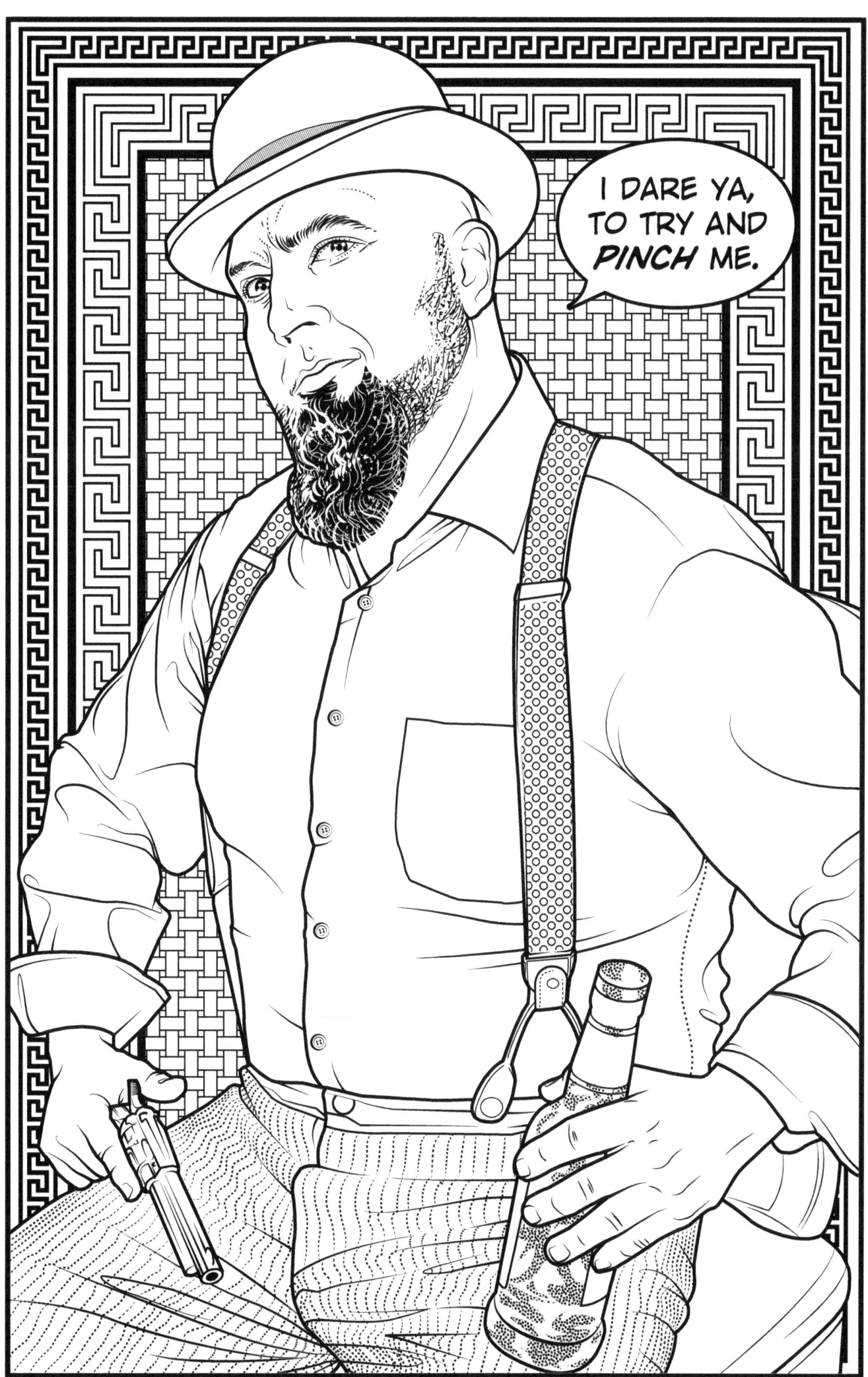

Merman Resting

Model: Proteus Waterflame

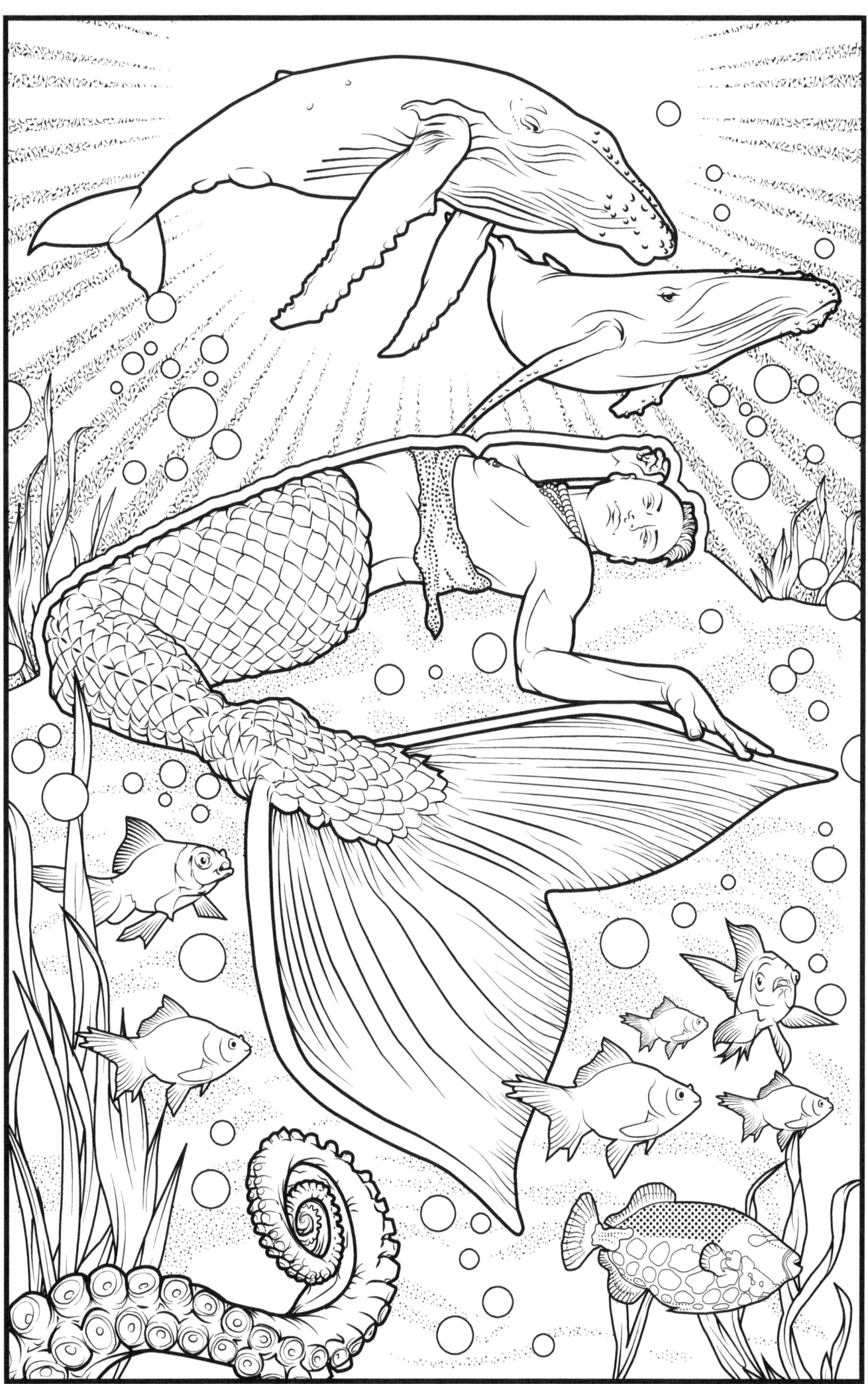

The Rigger
Model: JD of Two Knotty Boys

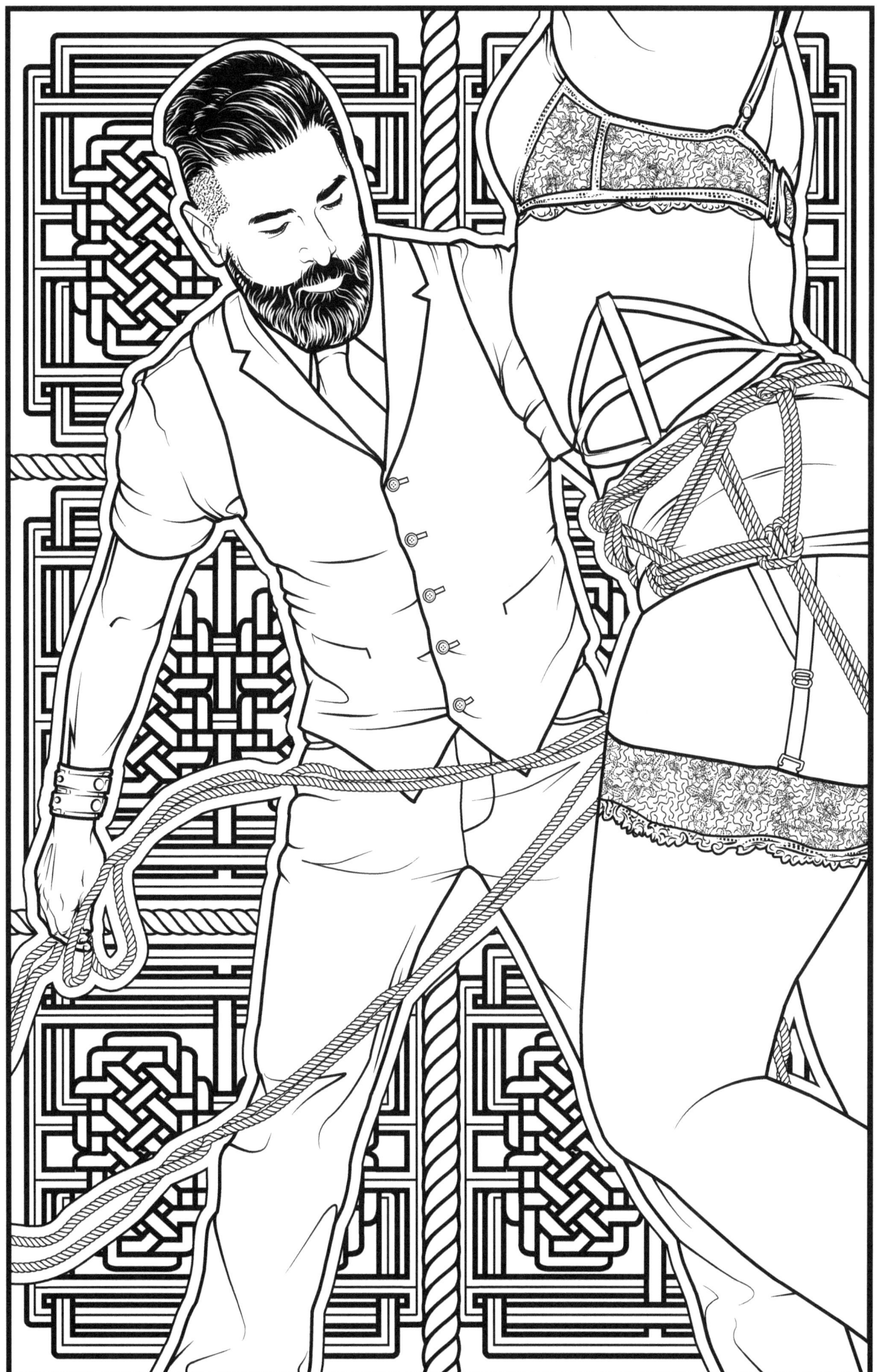

Jester

Models: Ismael Acosta

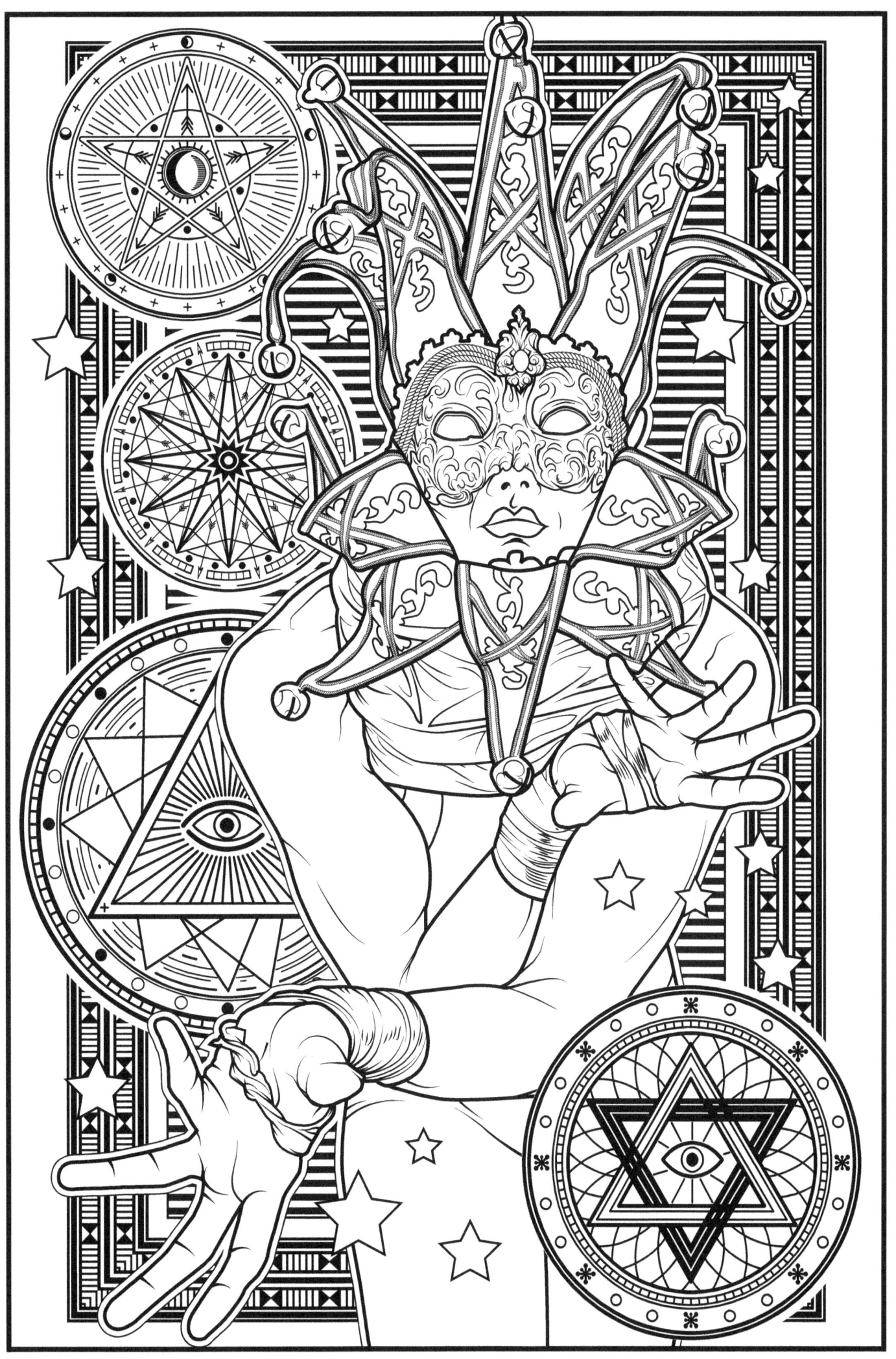

The Unicorn

Model: Ross Travis

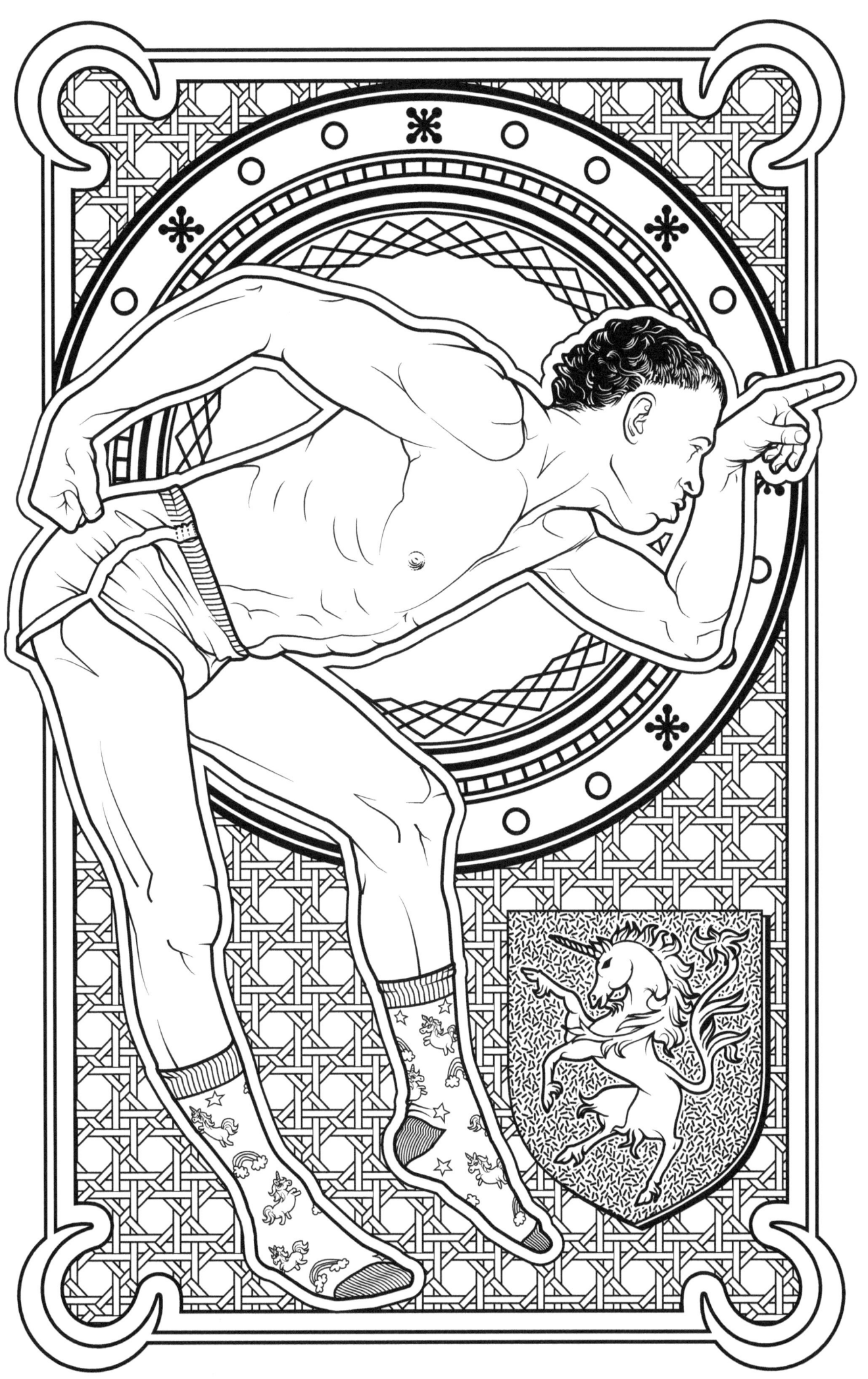

Bite Me Buffy

Model: Jesi Ringofire

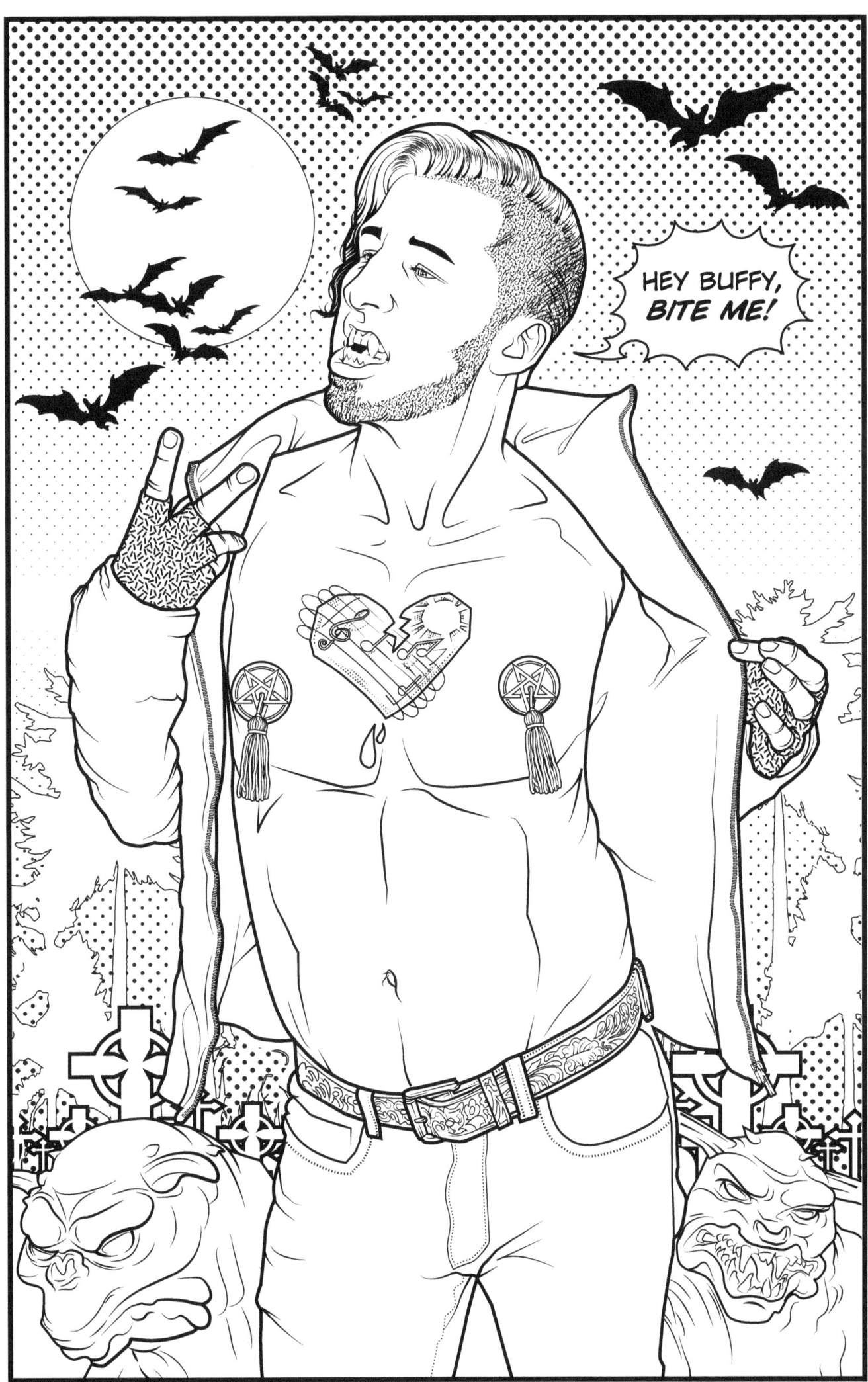

The Jewel Of Middle Earth

Model: Queer Al Skankovic

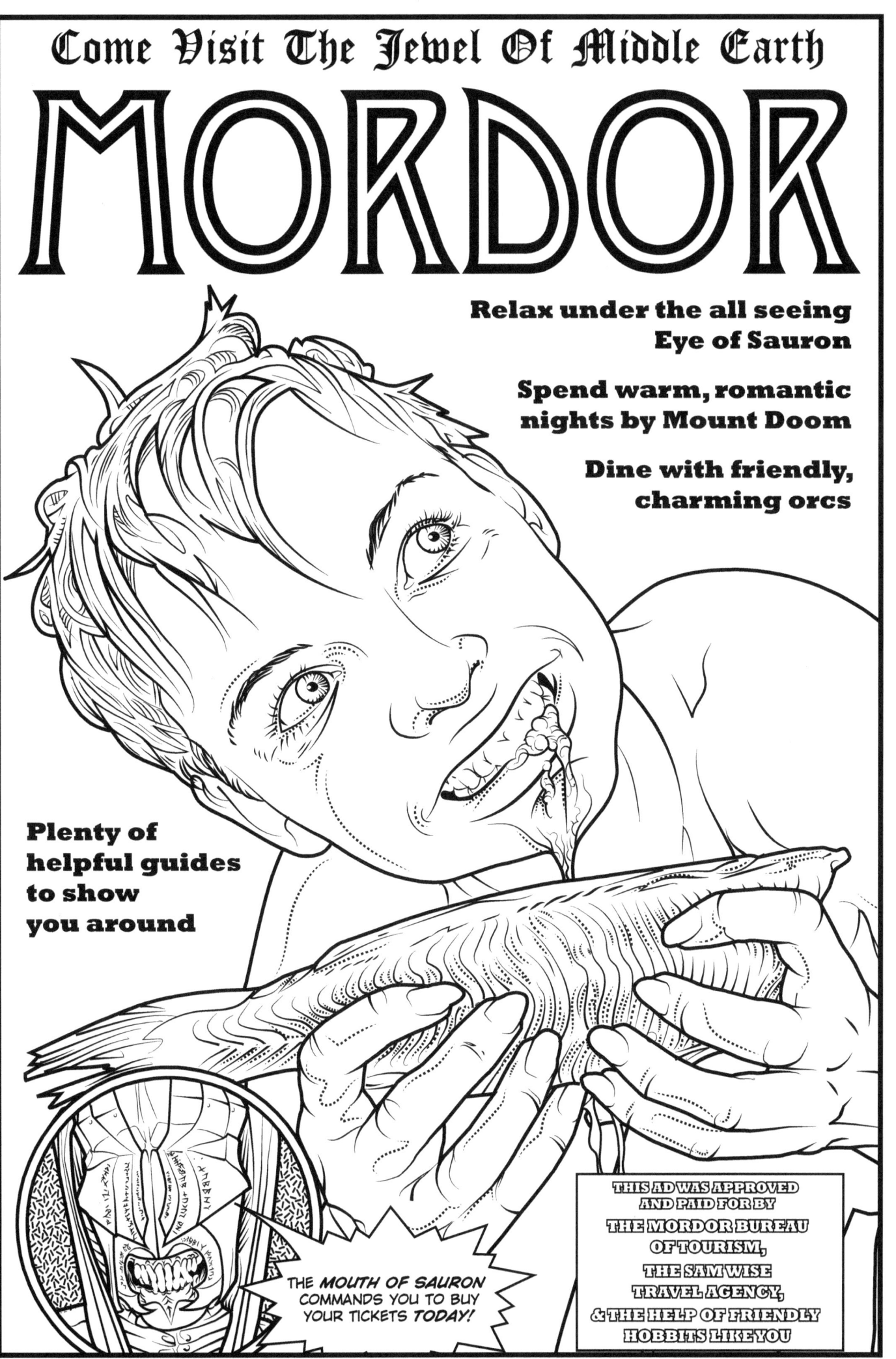

Shore Leave

Model: Sugar Buns

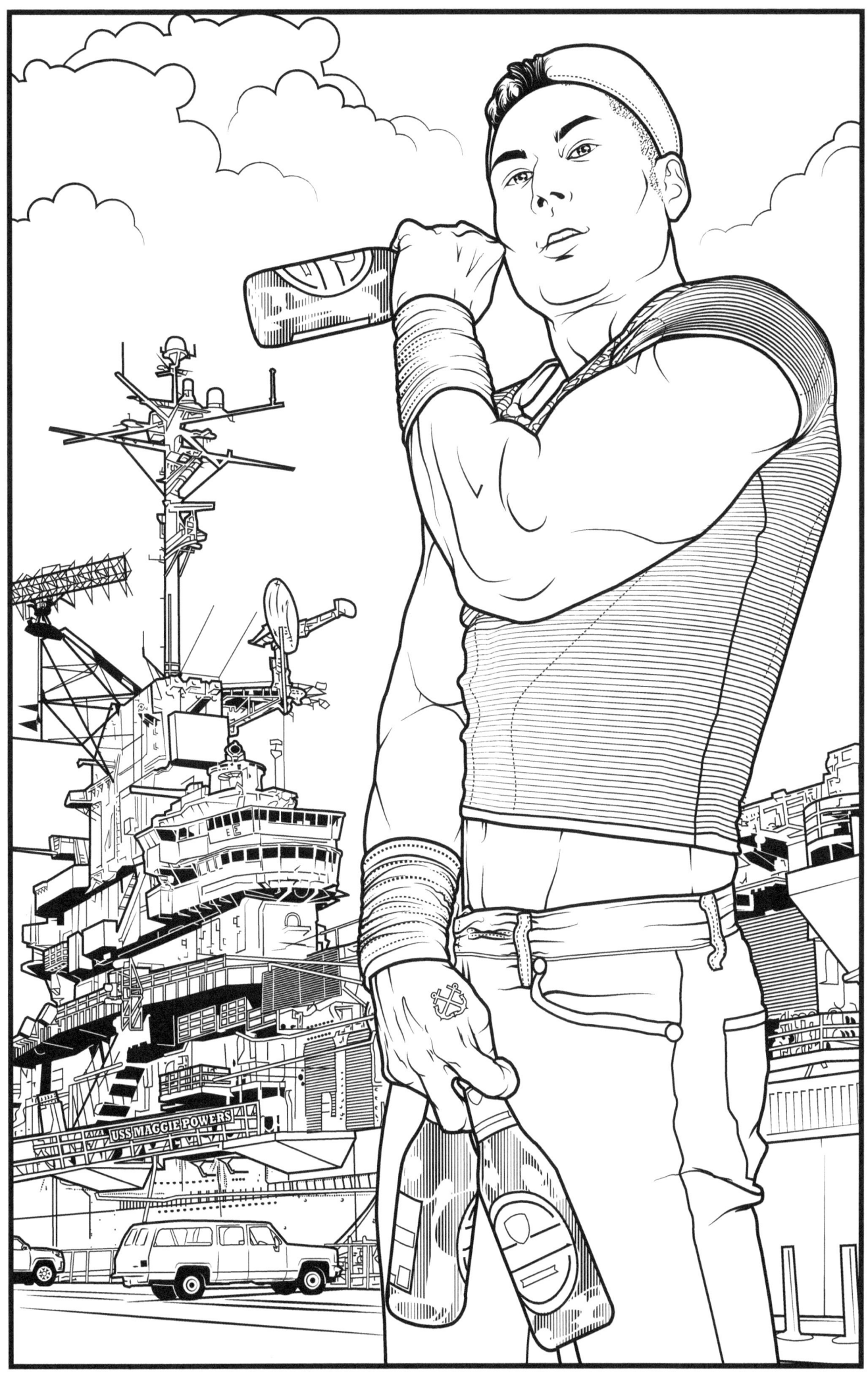

When The Joke's On You?

Model: Twitch

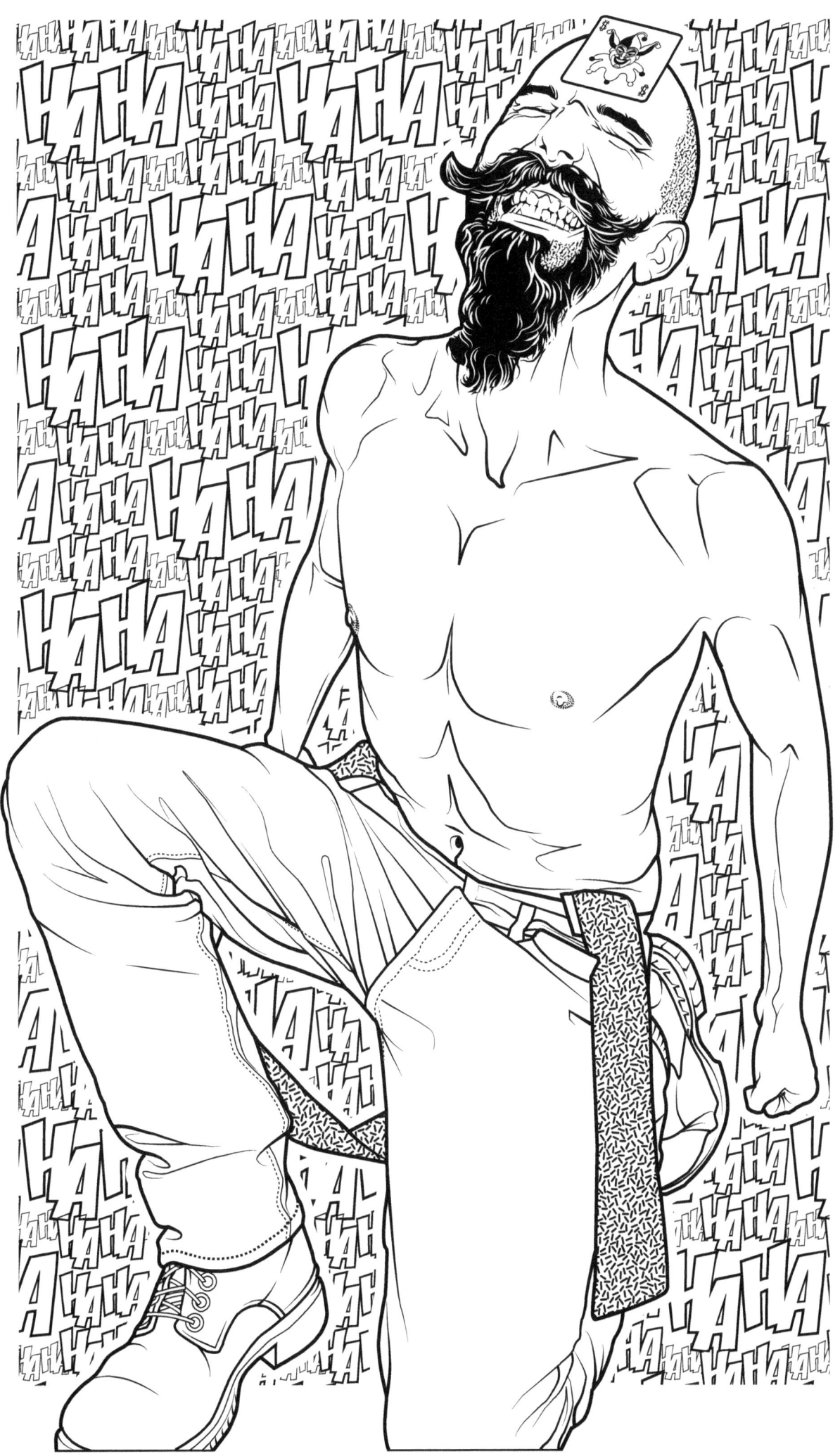

The Whip

Model: Matthew James

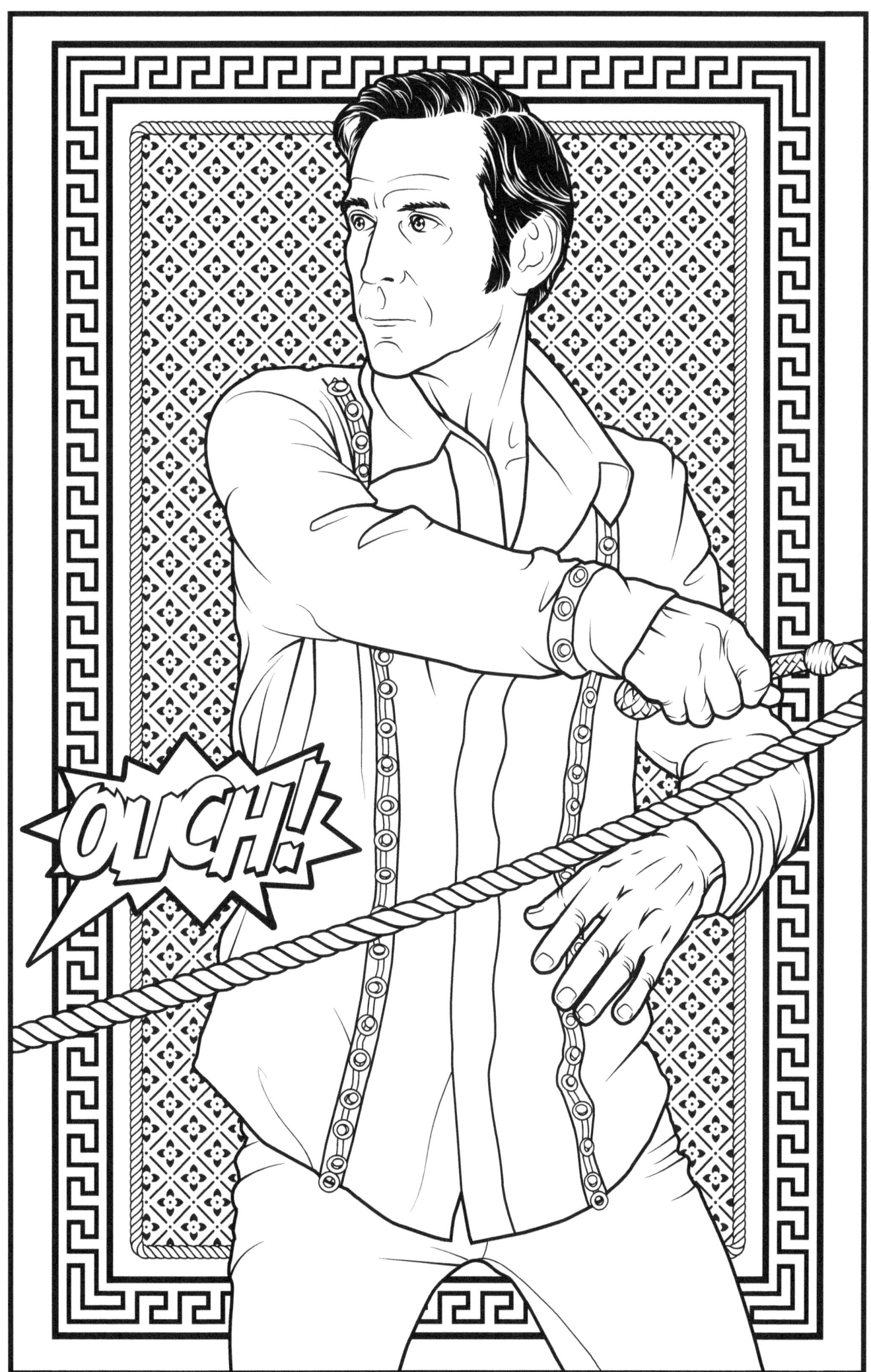

Daddy's Girls

Models: HisDame, Corrupt Morals & Greyish

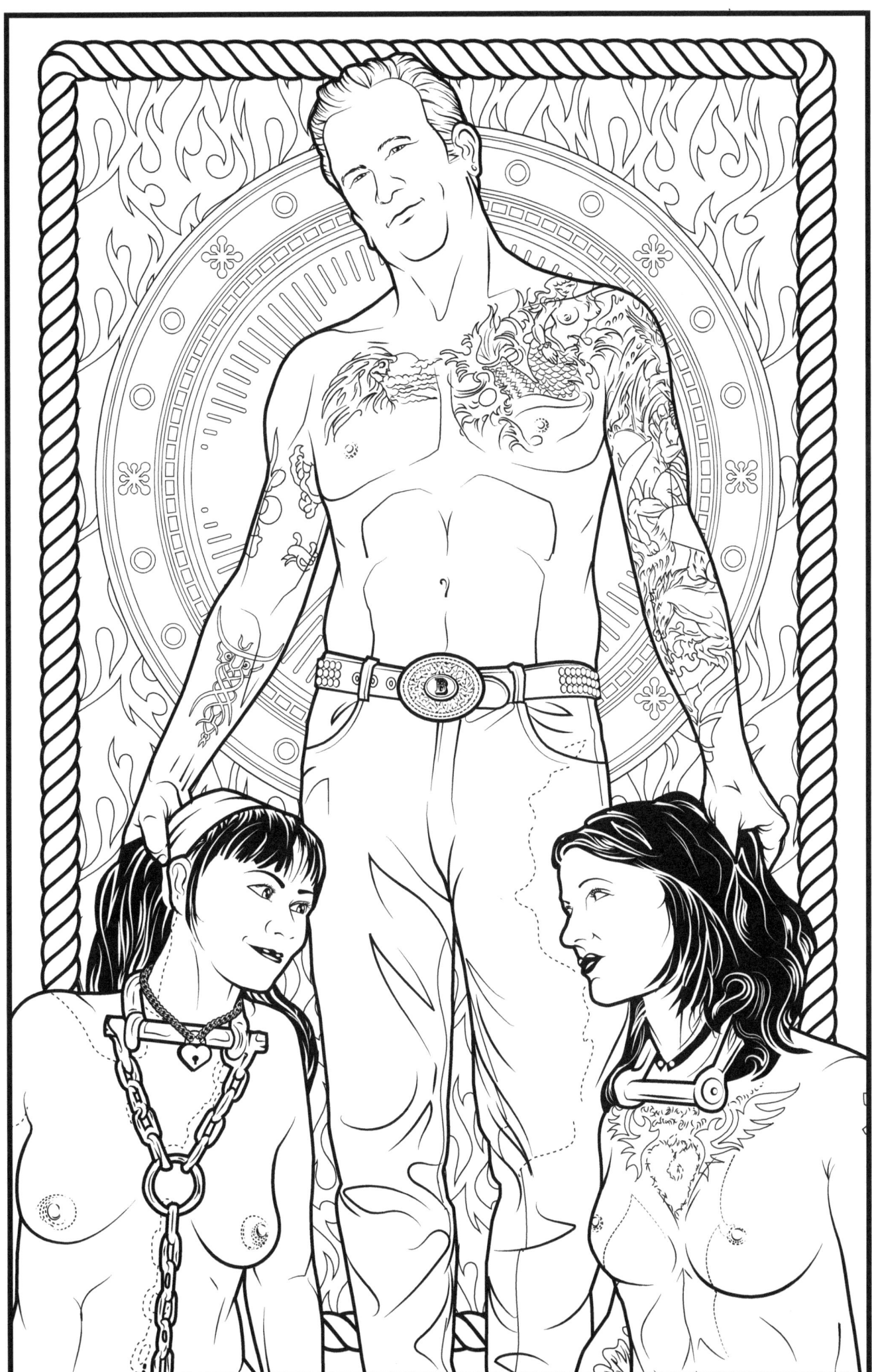

Floggers

Model: Alexander_Lucard

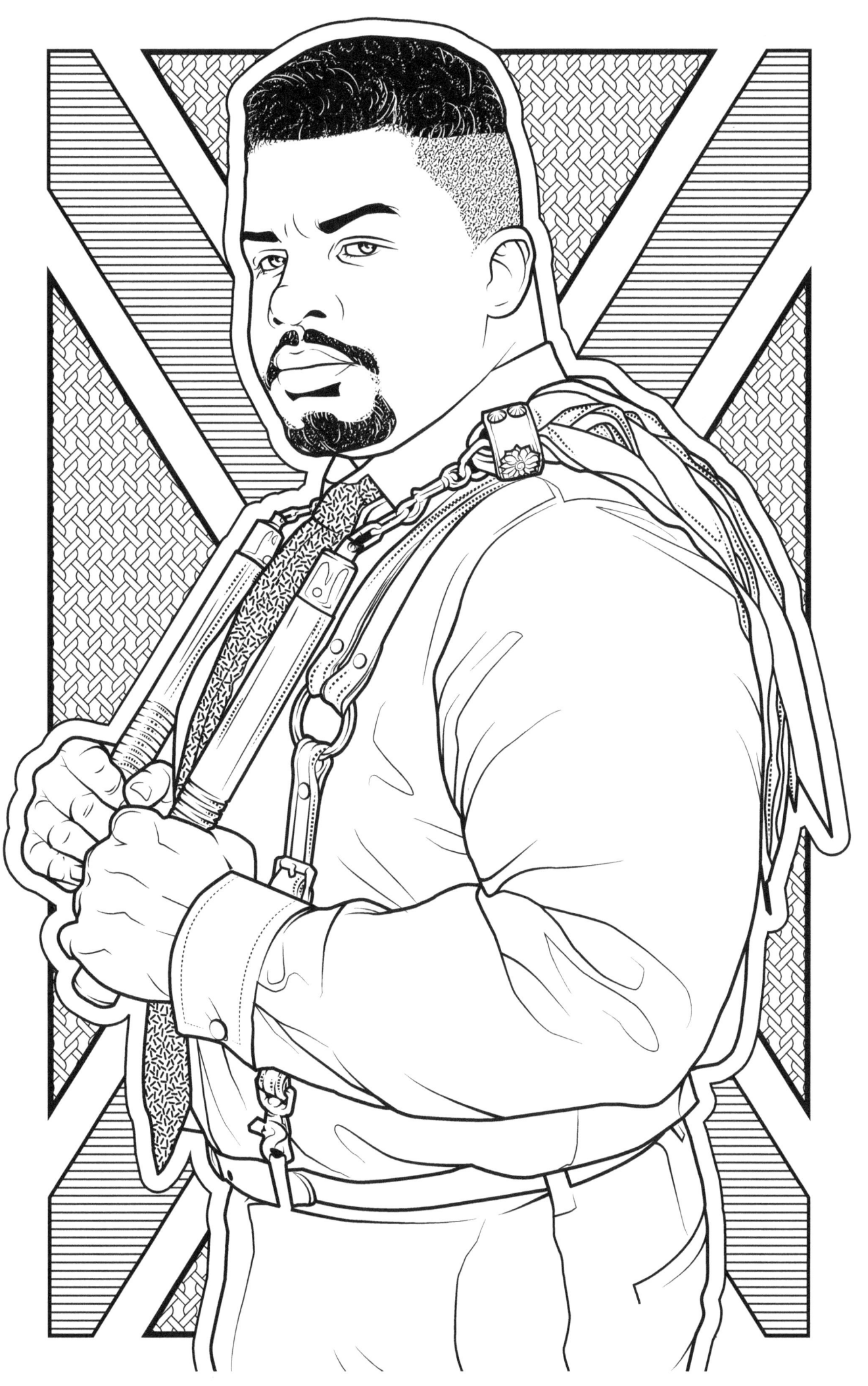

Busy Bee

Model: Jet Noir

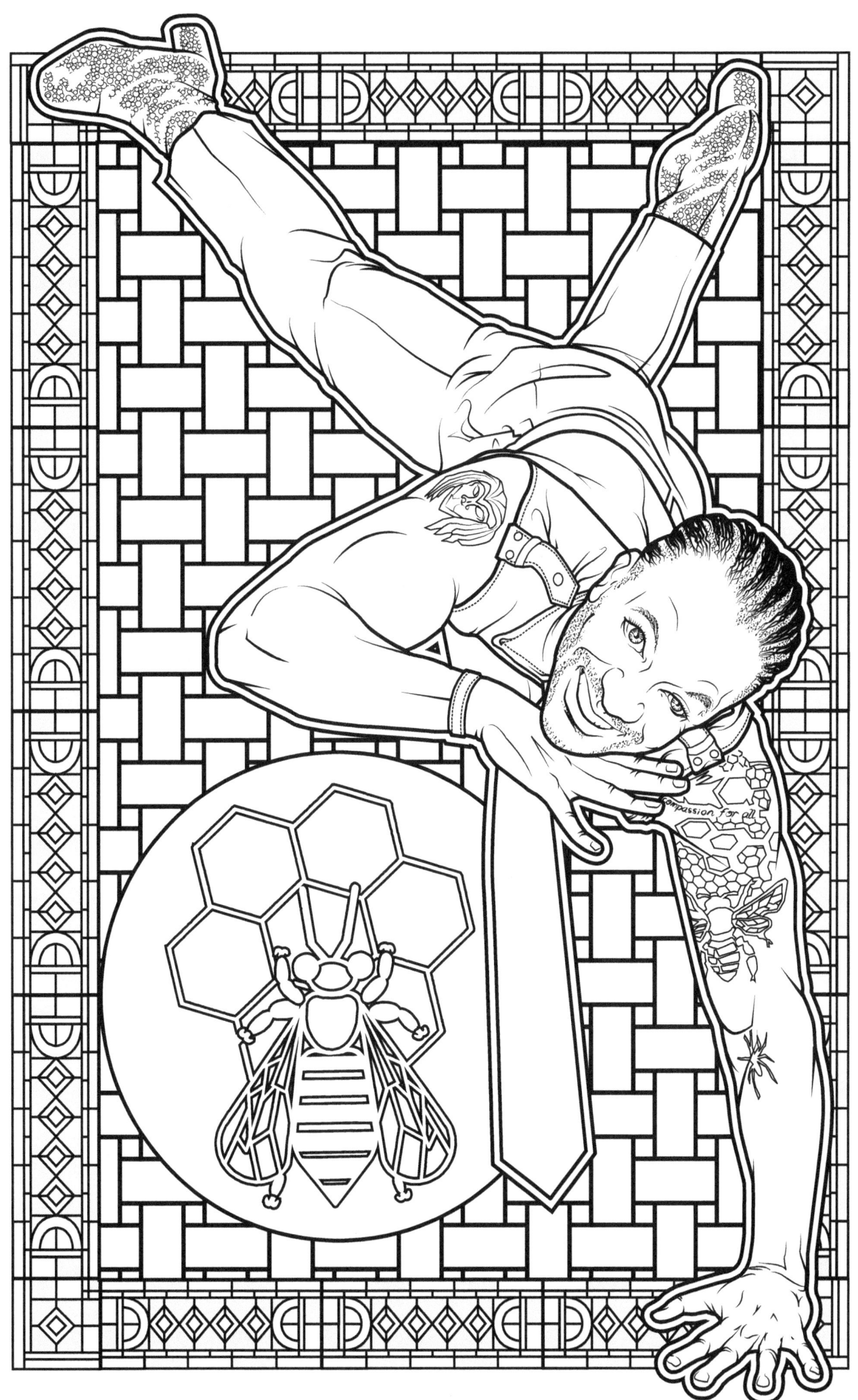

Music Of The Night

Models: Jeff Cathcart and Arcadia Kane

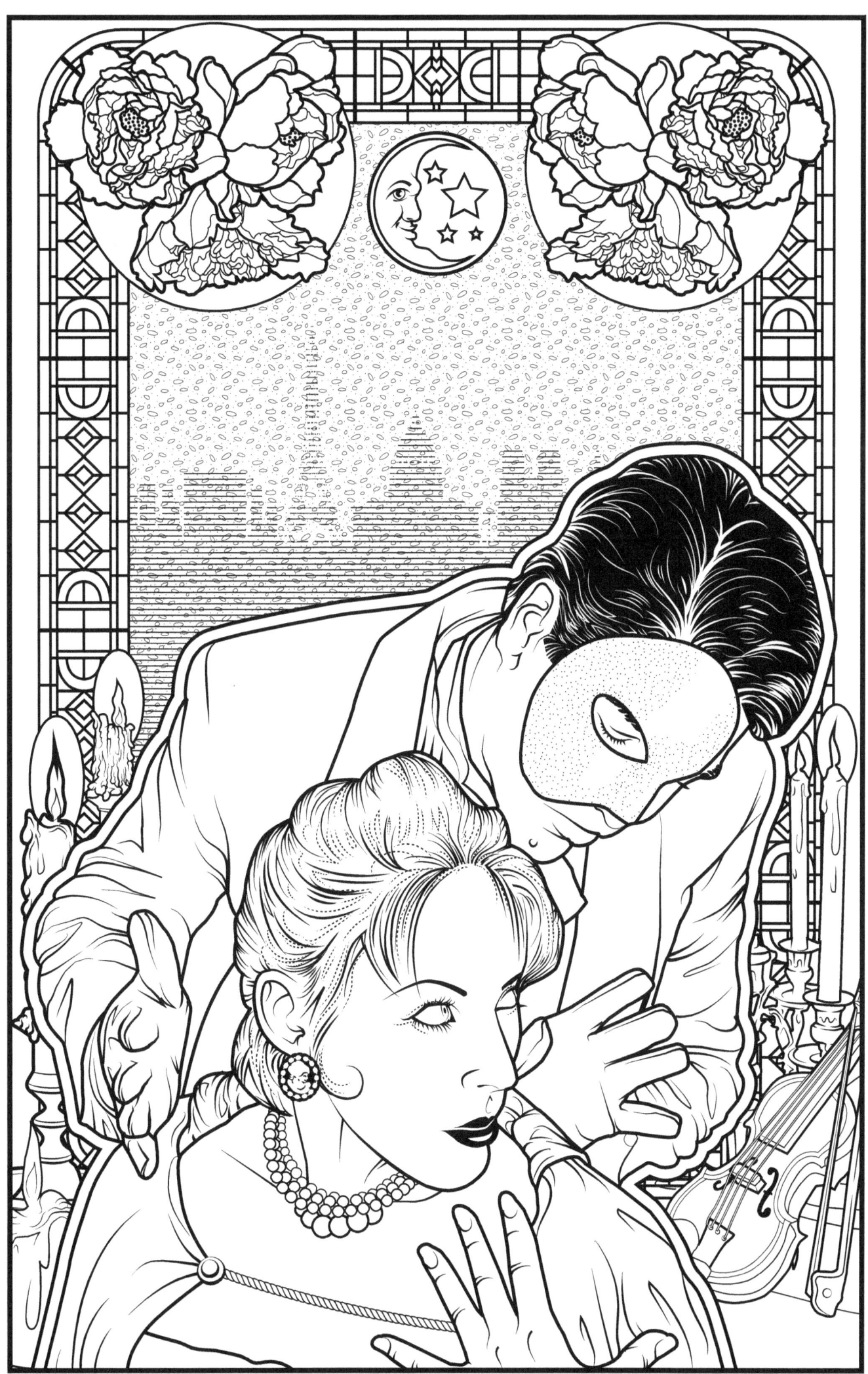

Steamwork

Model: Lee Harvey Roswell

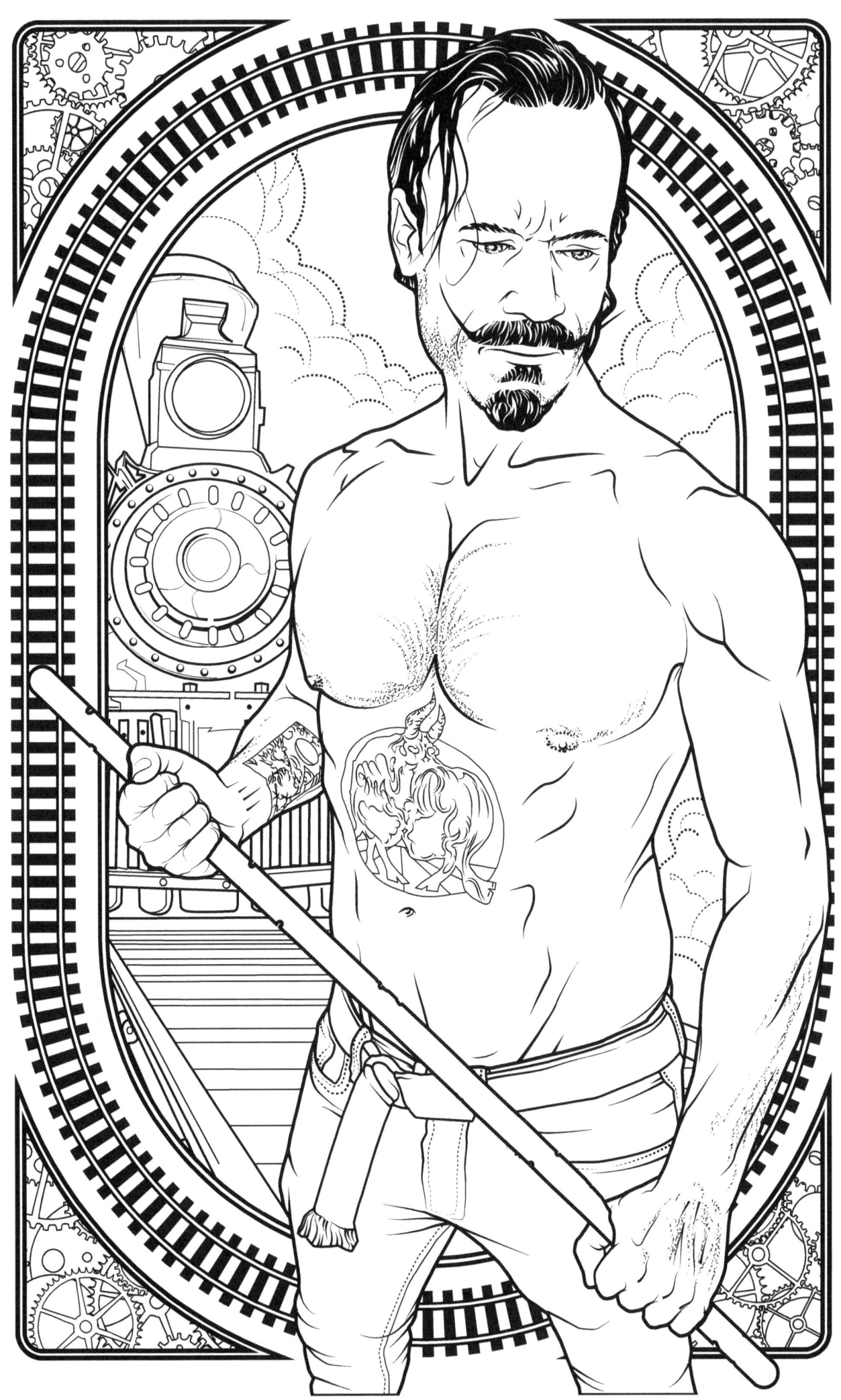

The Leap

Model: Ismael Acosta

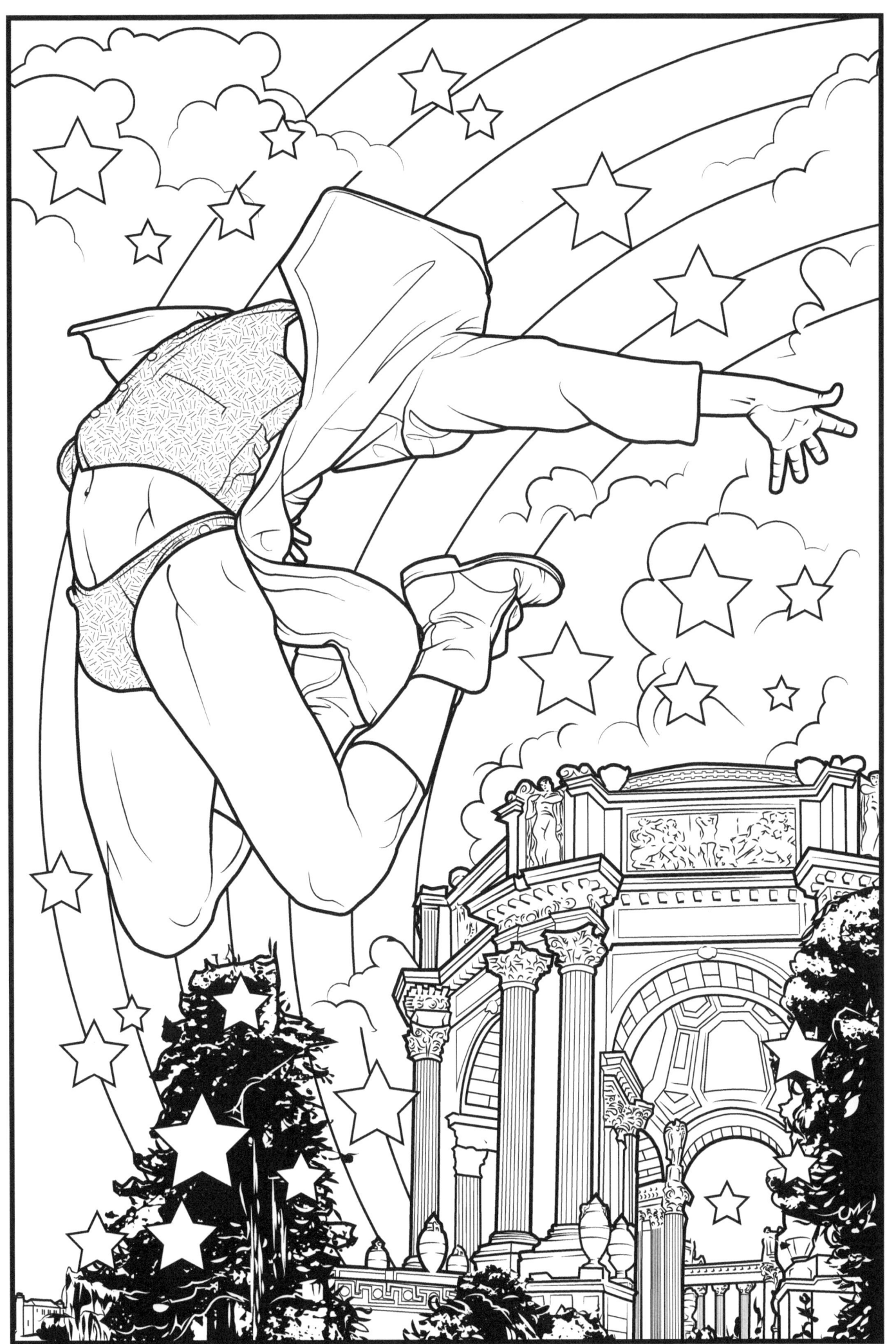

The Prince

Model: Shakey Gibson

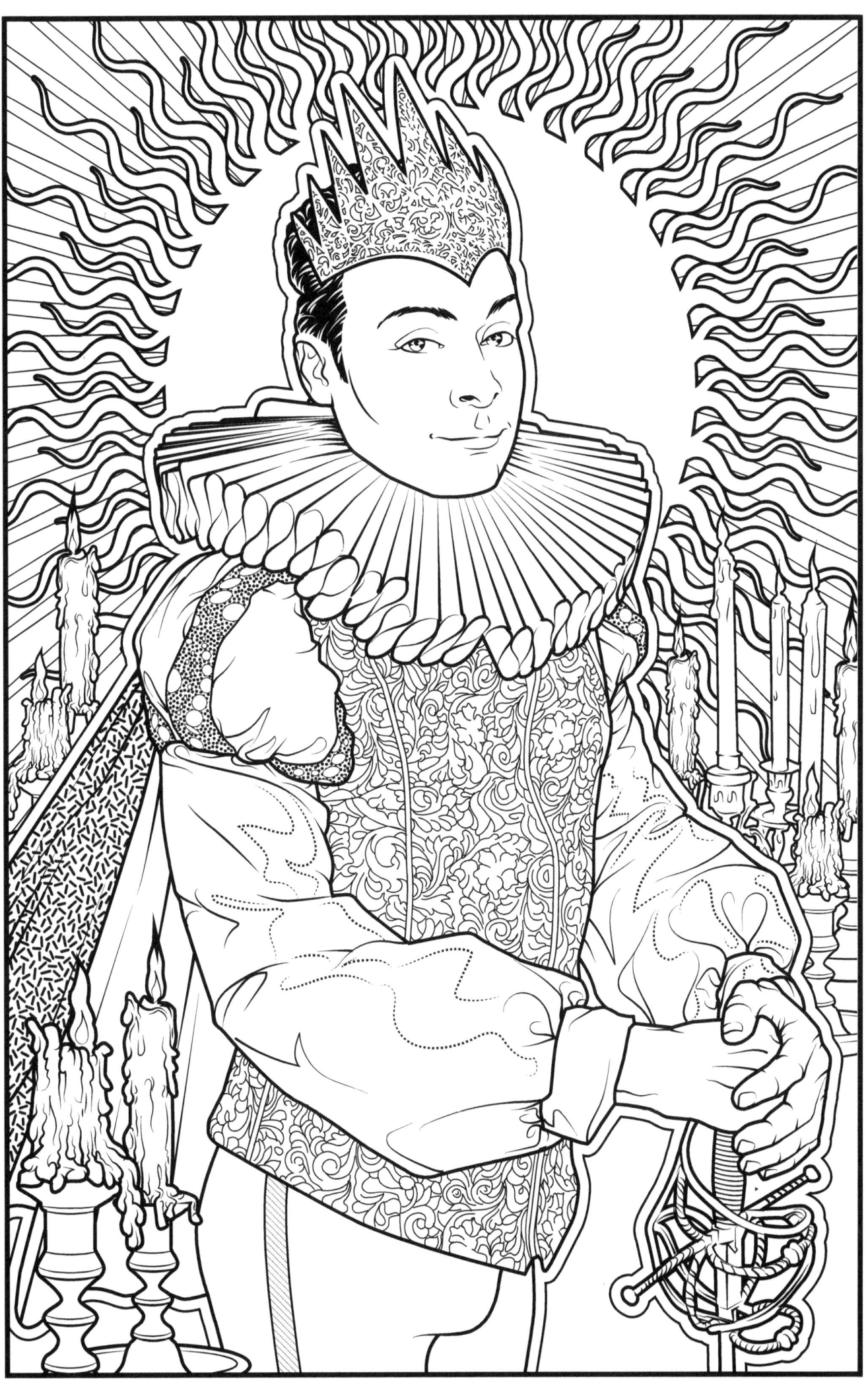

Magic Elixir

Model: Benjamin Wester

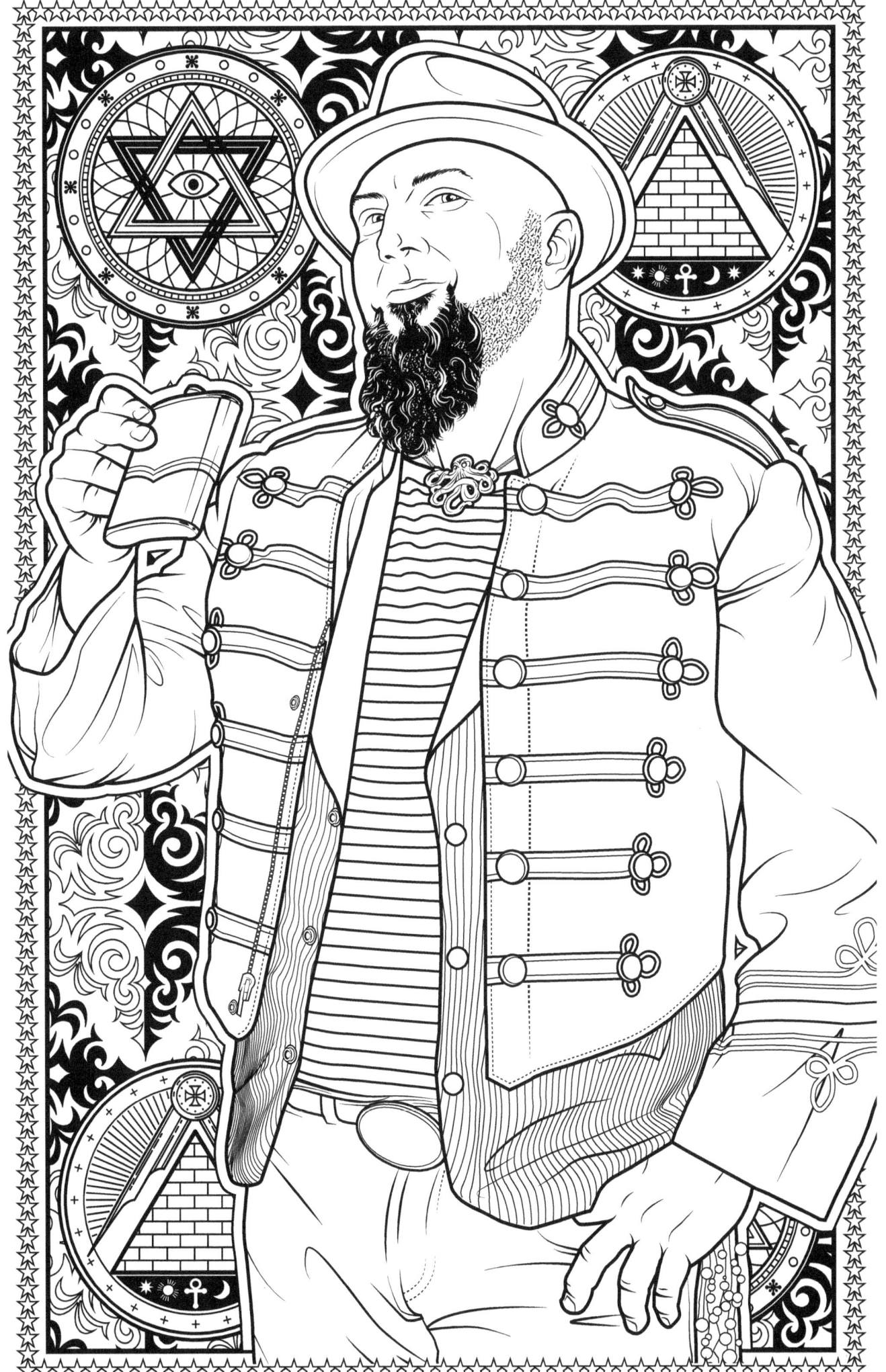

Drape

Model: Ismael Acosta

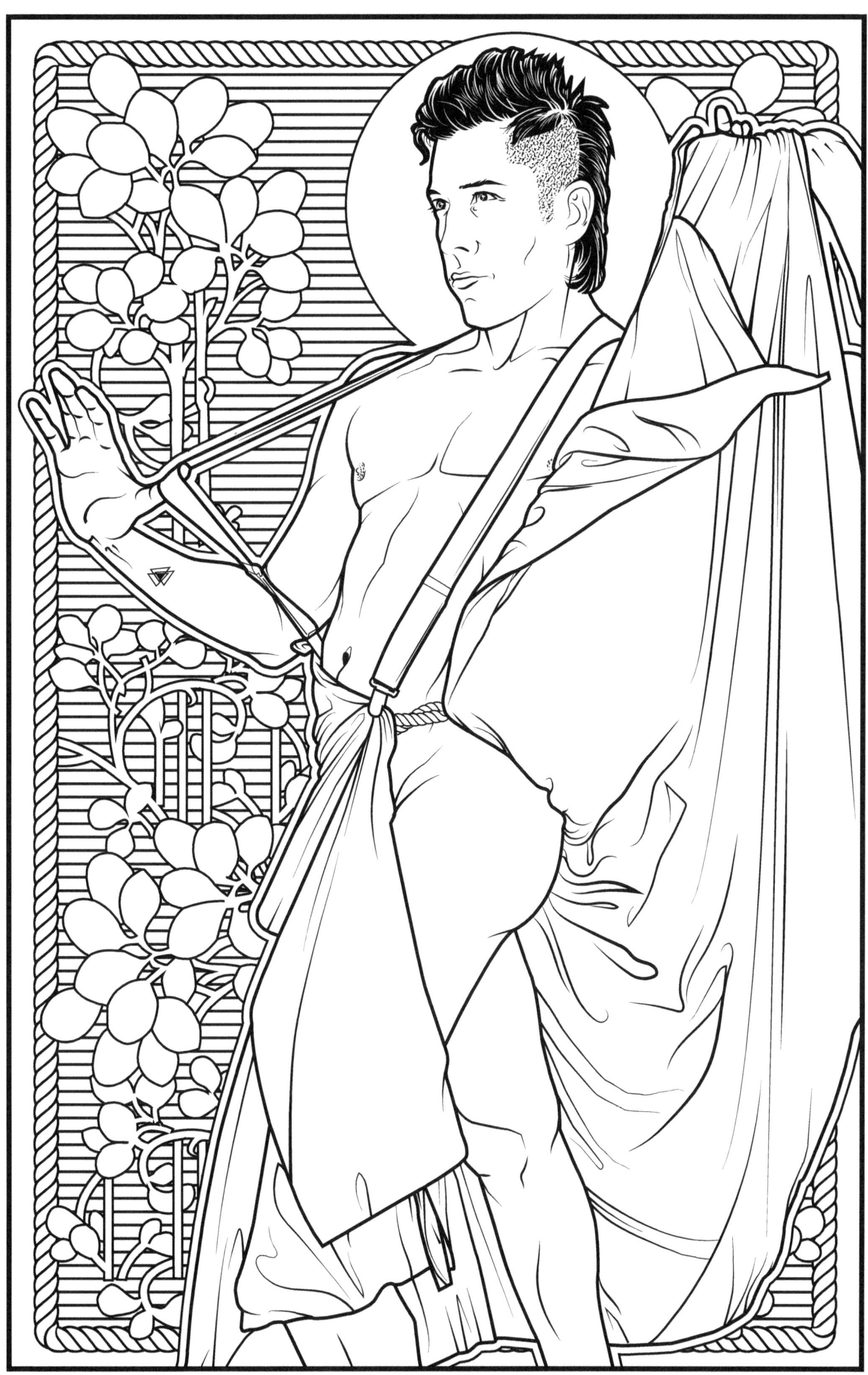

It's Good Being King

Model: Jim Sweeney aka Kingfish of Hubba Hubba Revue

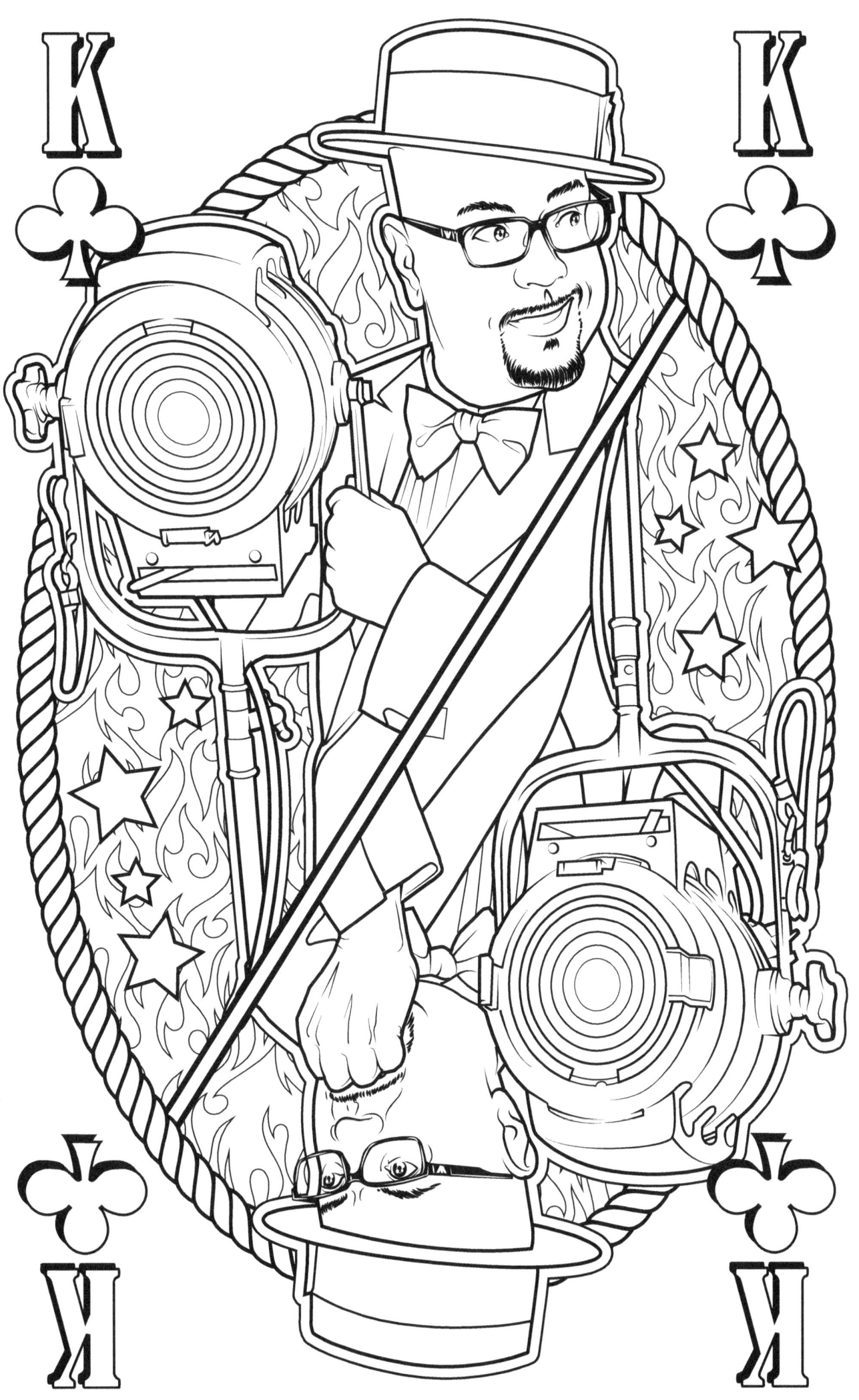

Rain and Chris

Models: Rain DeGrey and Chris,

hosts of Dirty Talk After Hours Podcast

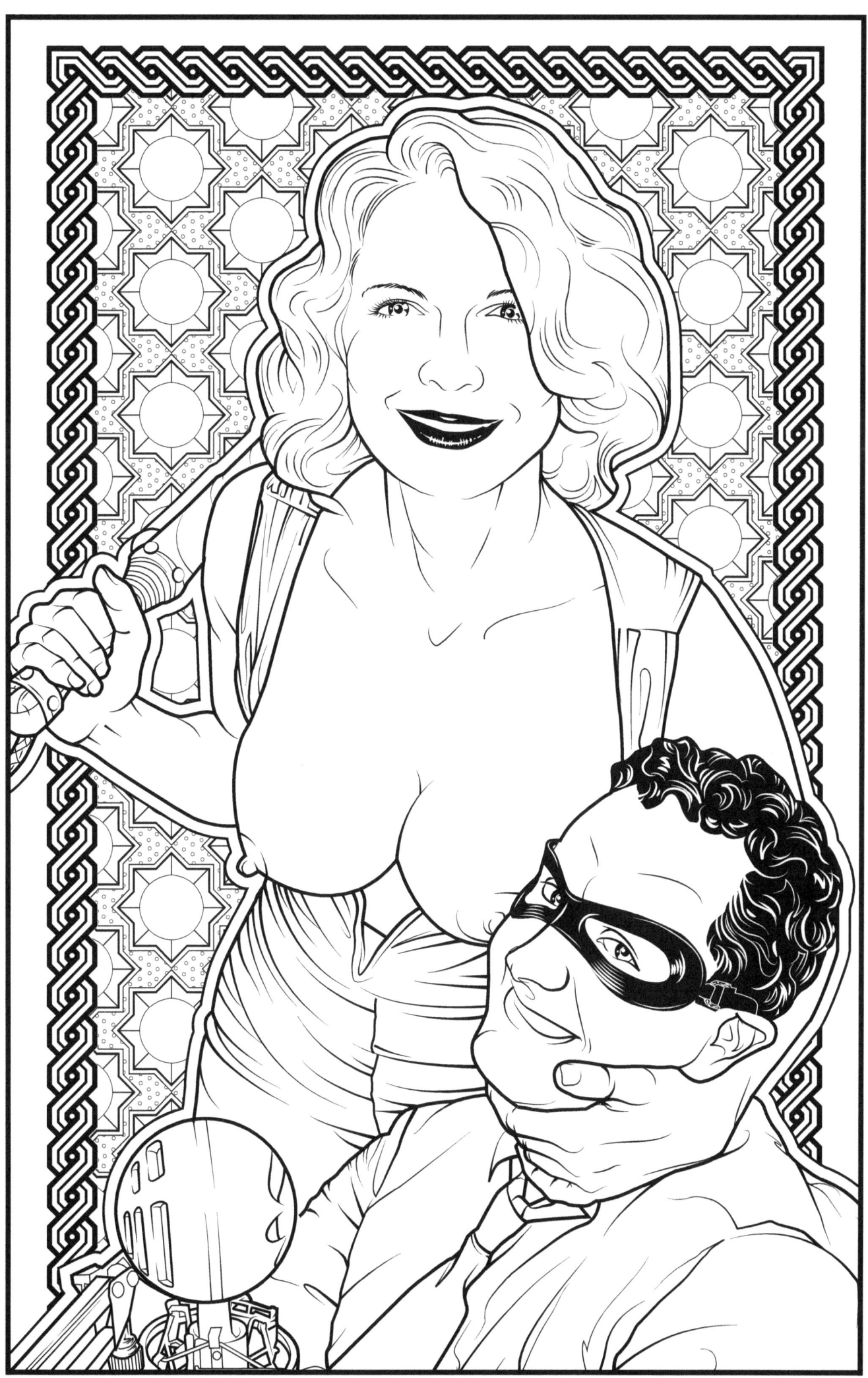

Scotland Forever

Model: Jeff Cathcart

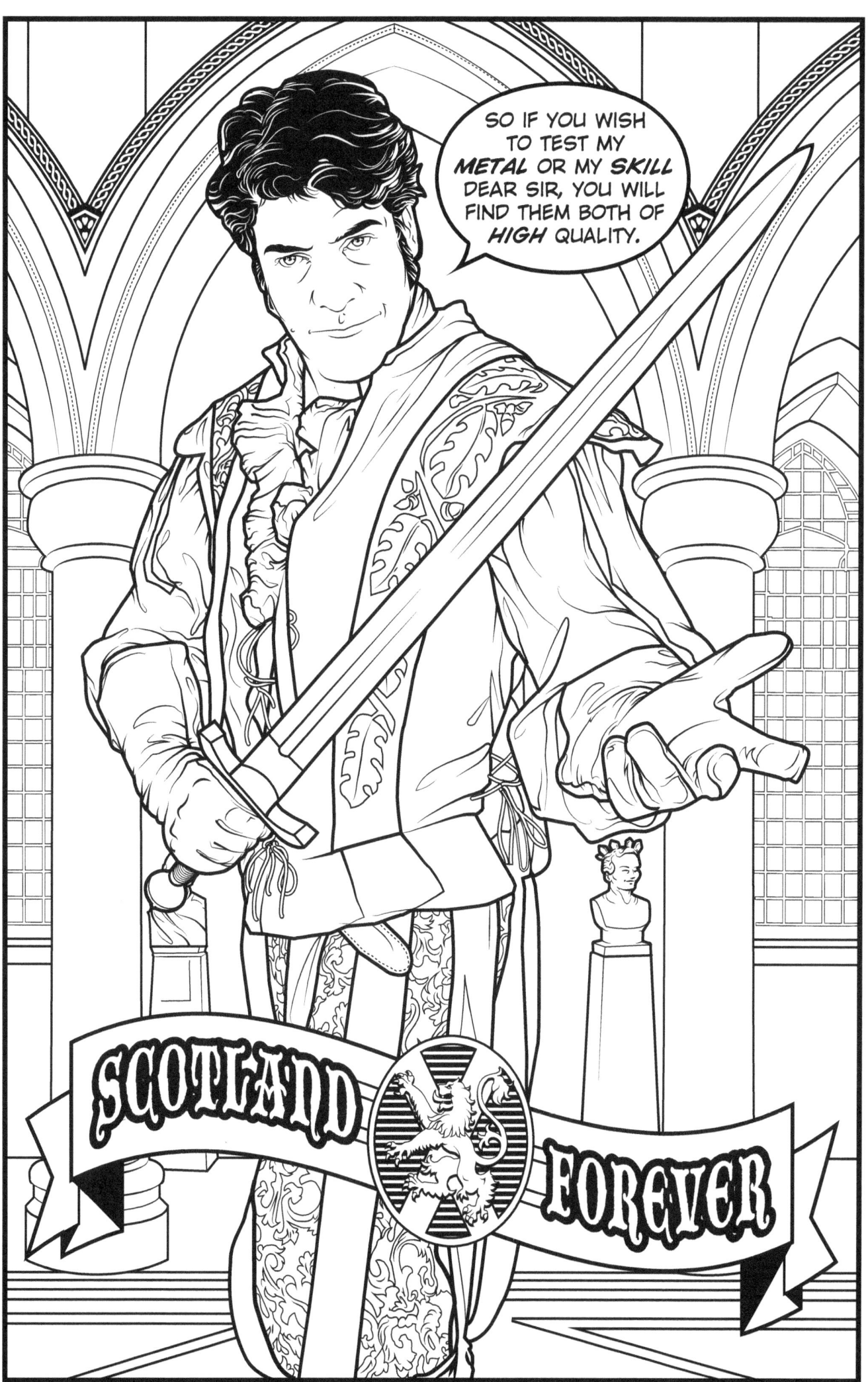

Booty call

Model: Guy Vigor

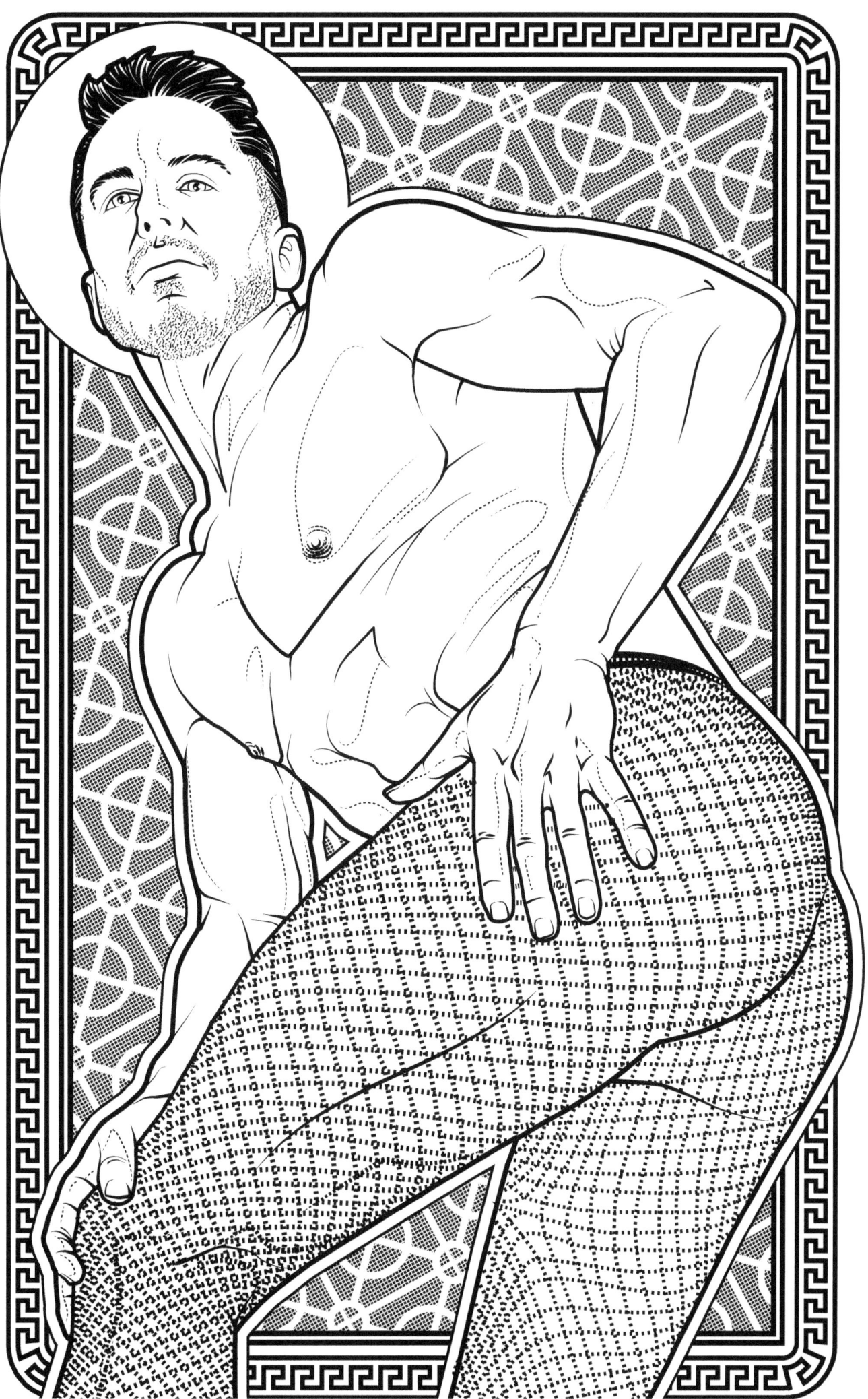

No Clowning Around

Models: Major Suttle-Tease & Charlie Duneaux

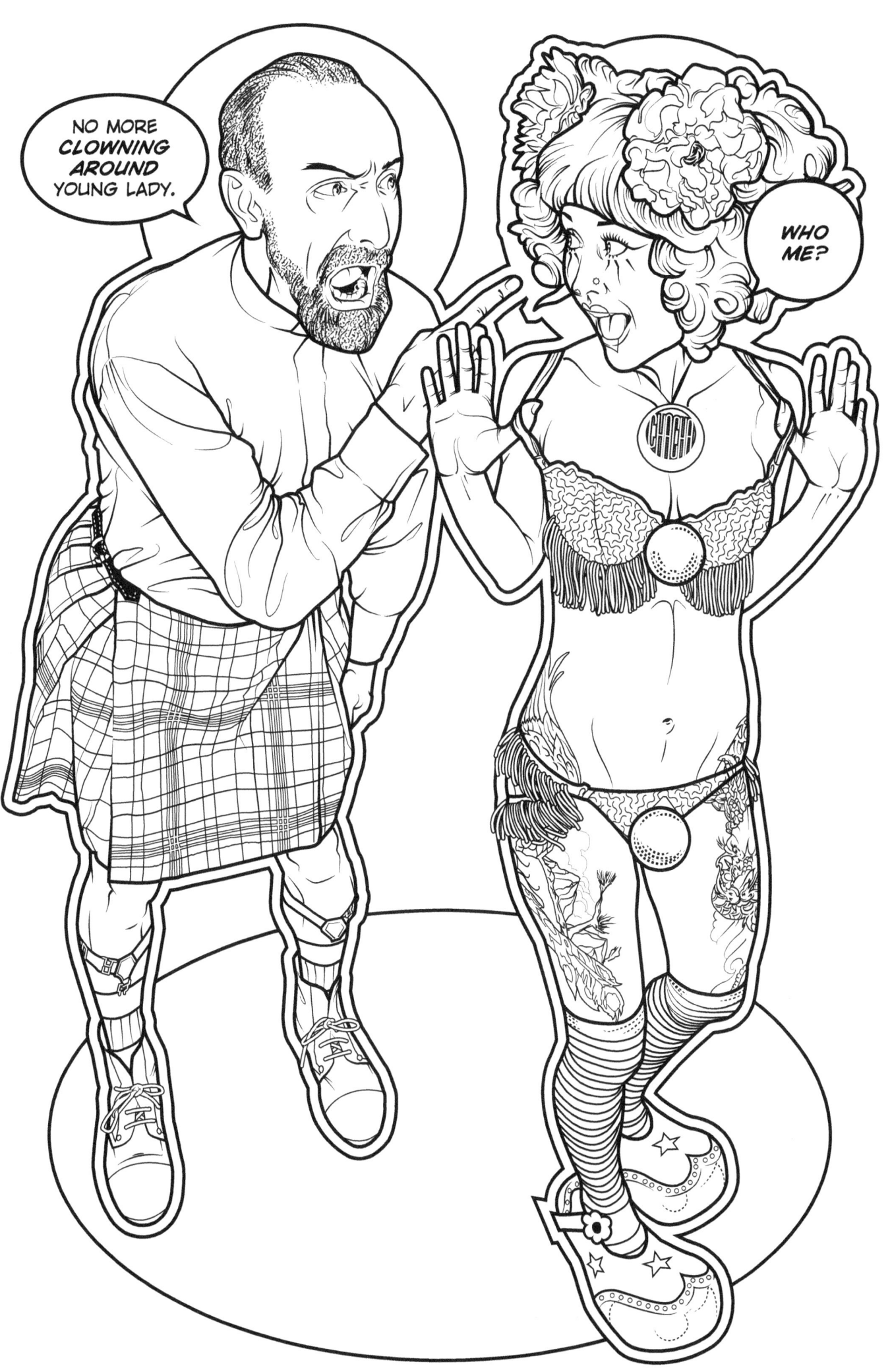

Trevor's Back

Model: Trevor

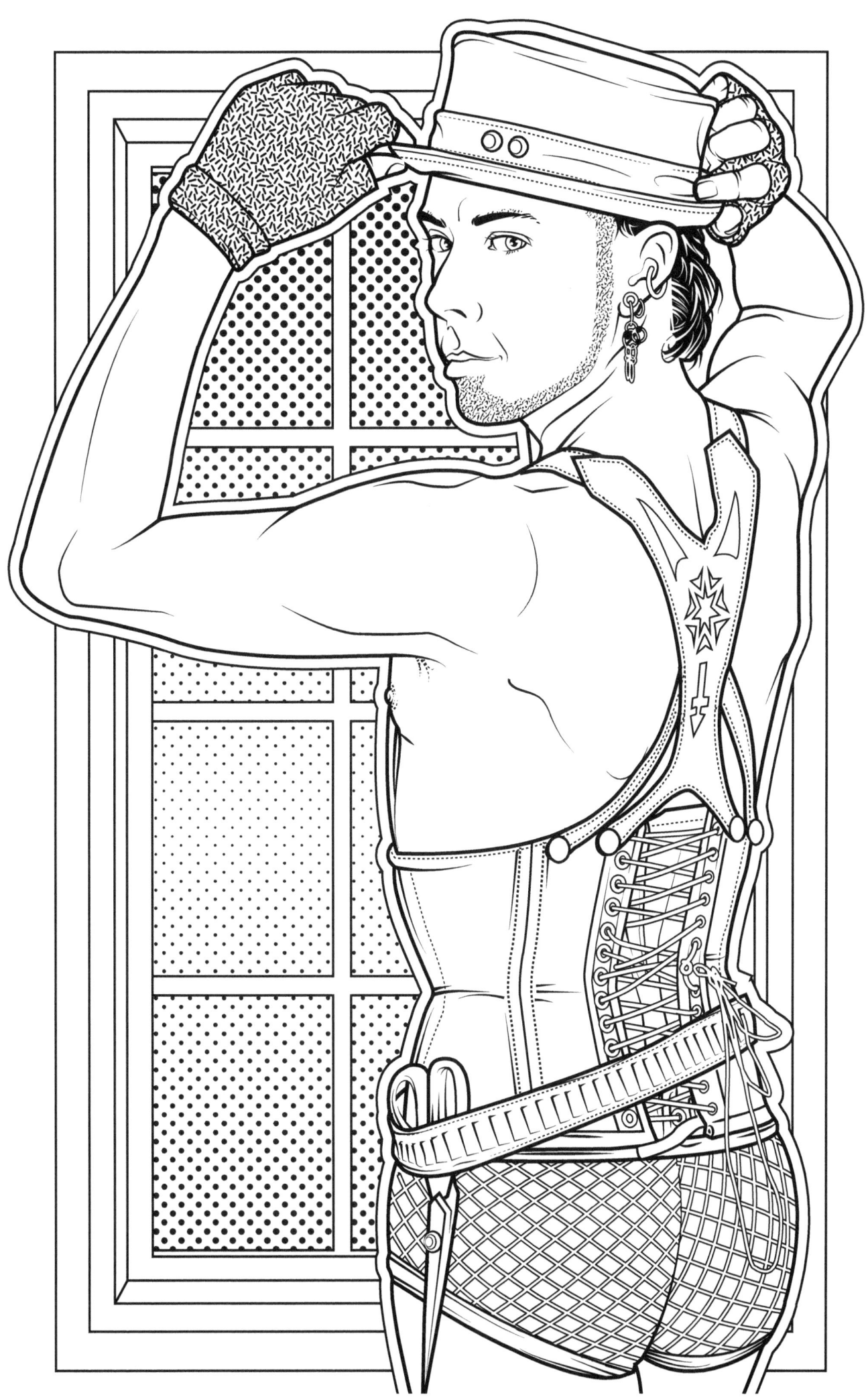

Dan The Man

Model: Dan of Two Knotty Boys and Kitty Meow

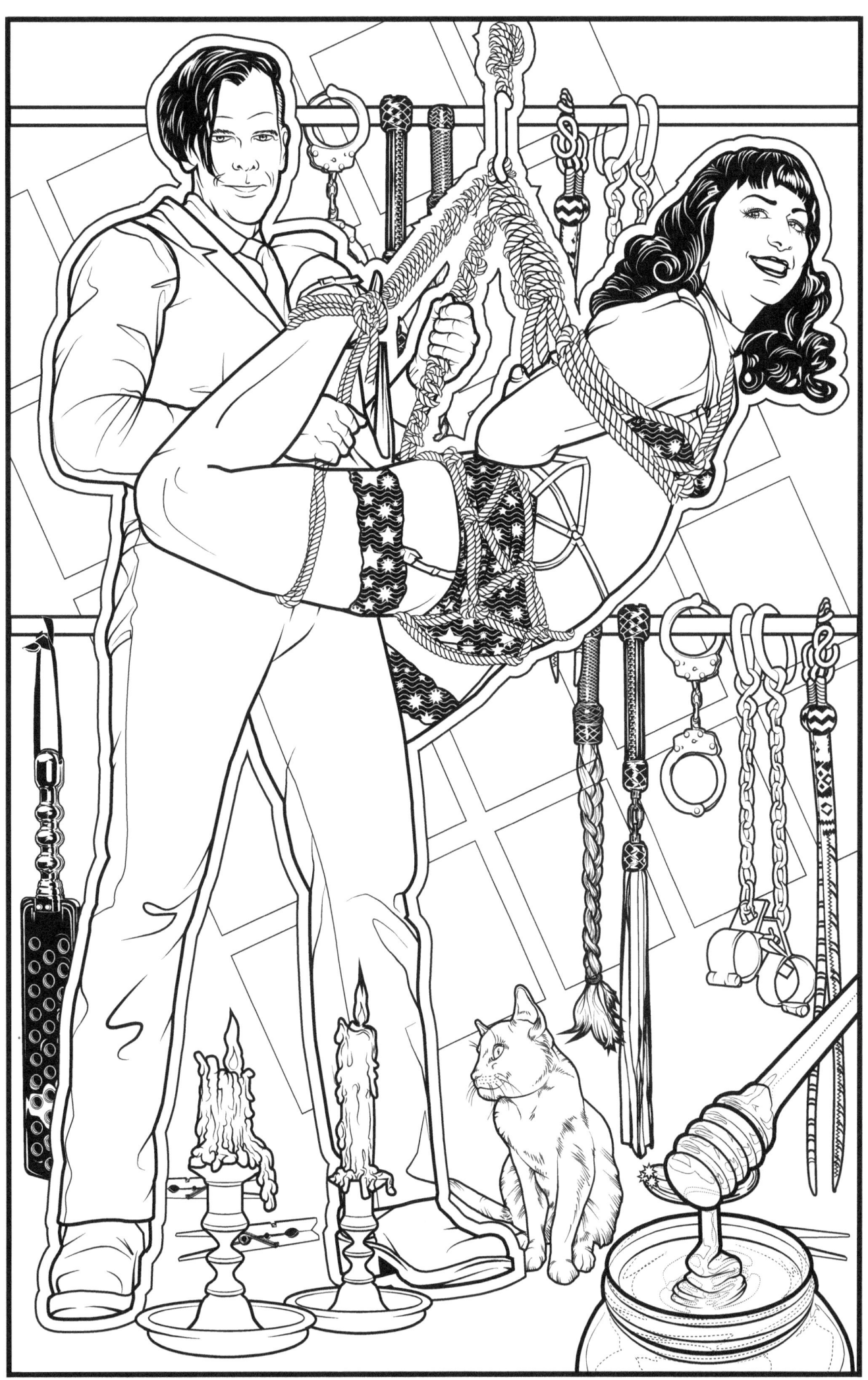

Grab Ass

Model: Aurora Rose (with helping hands from Wonder Dave)

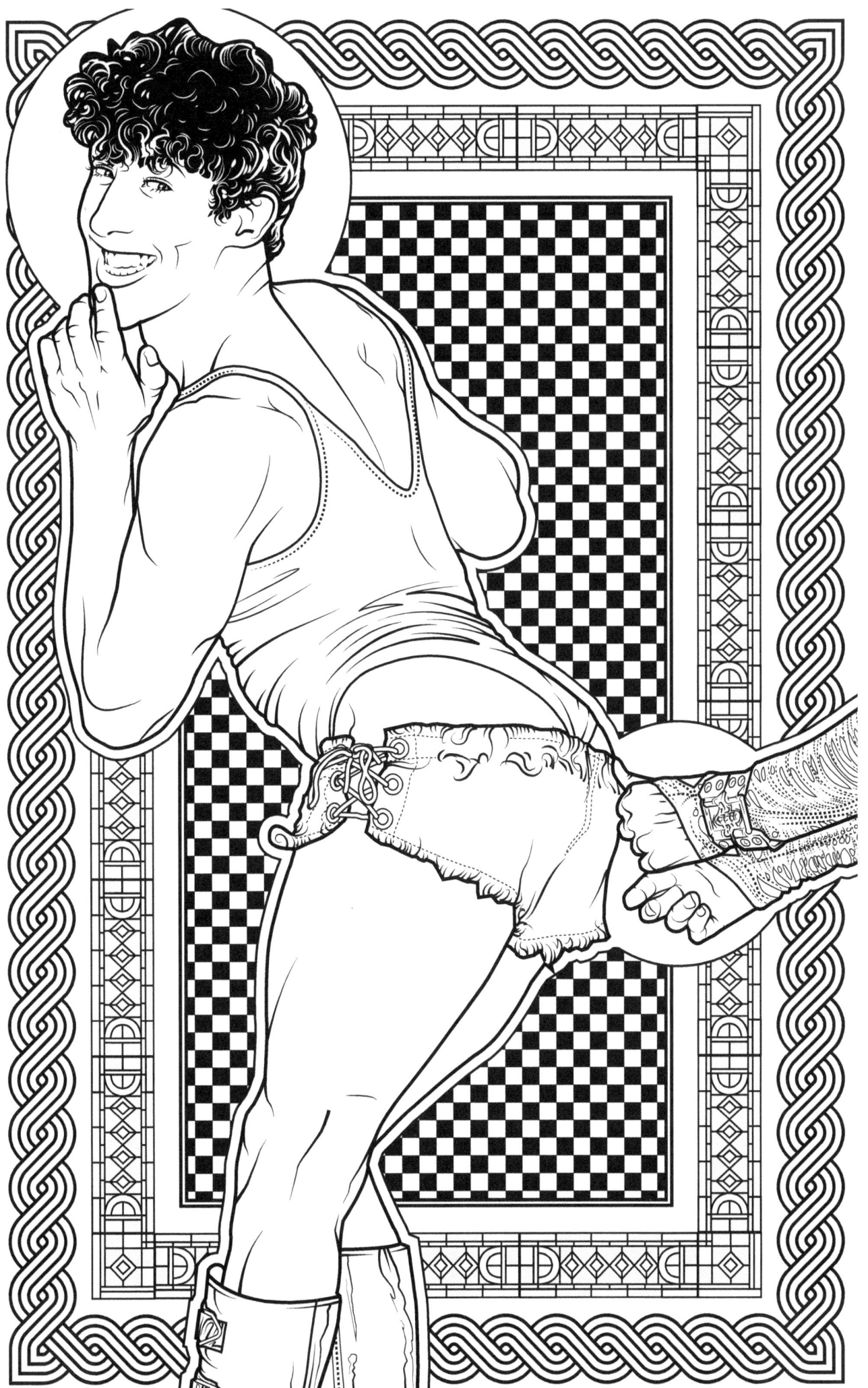

Ballet Dancer

Model: Ismael Acosta

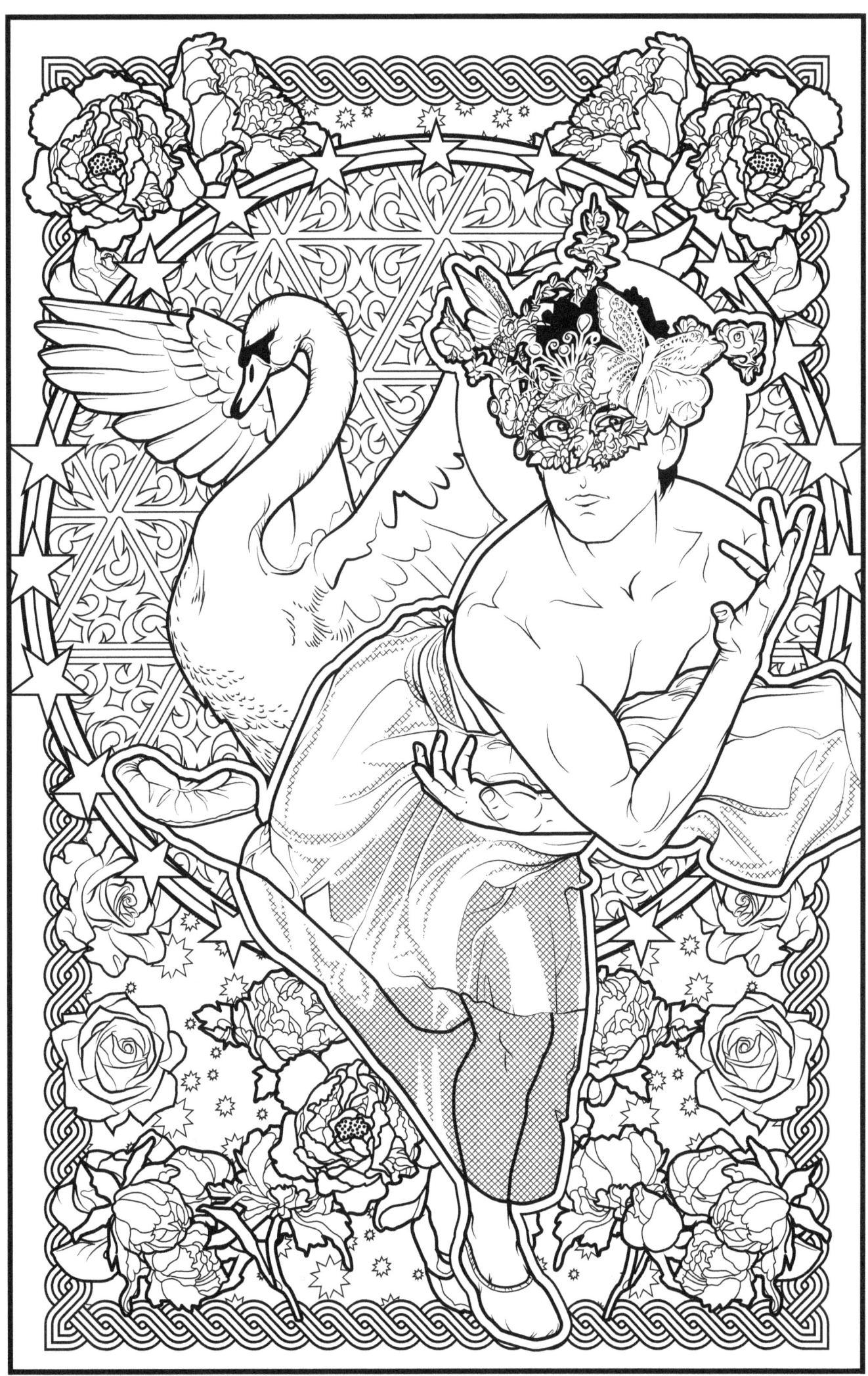

Trevor Magic

Model: Trevor

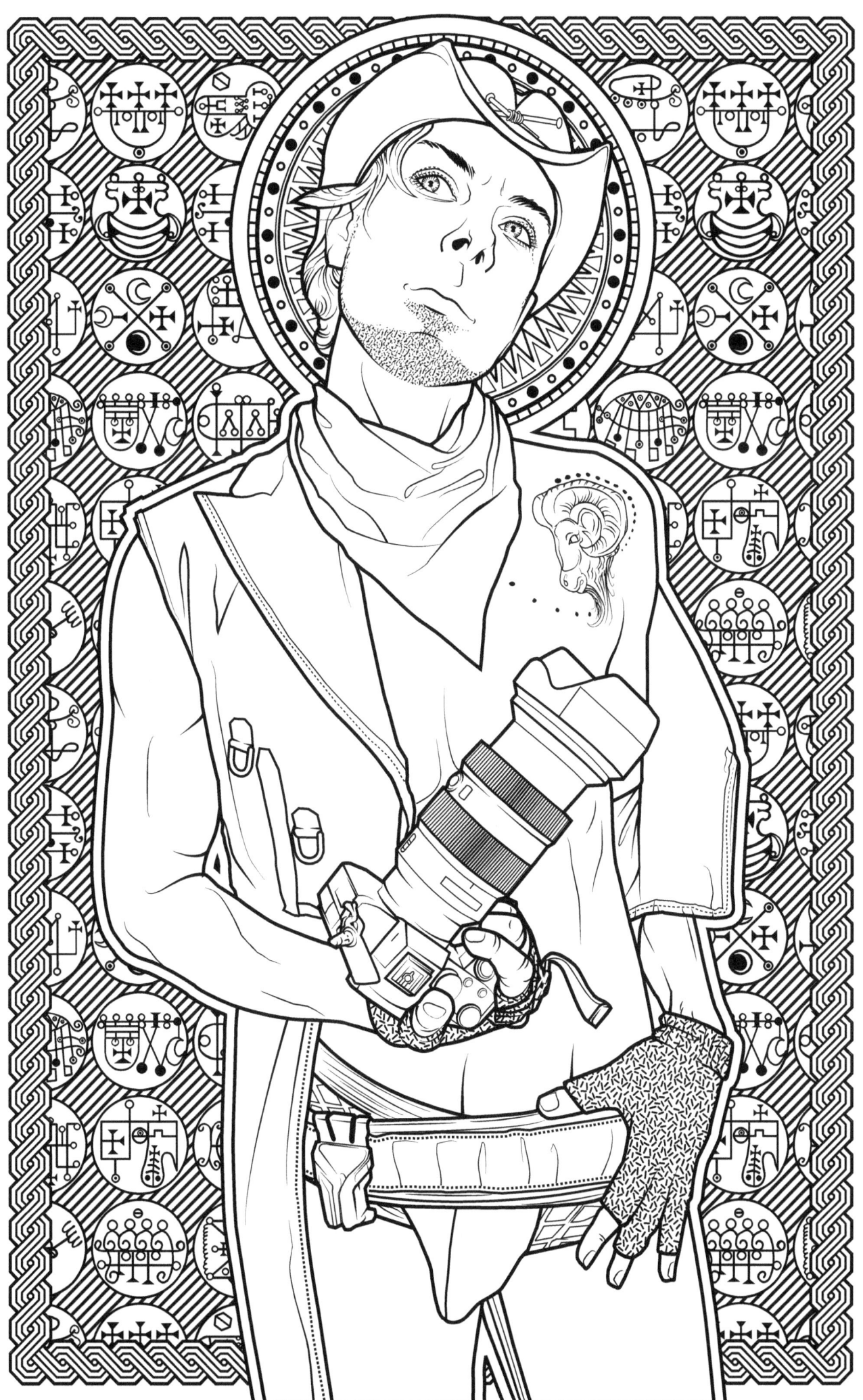

The Bunny-Man

Model: Guy Vigor

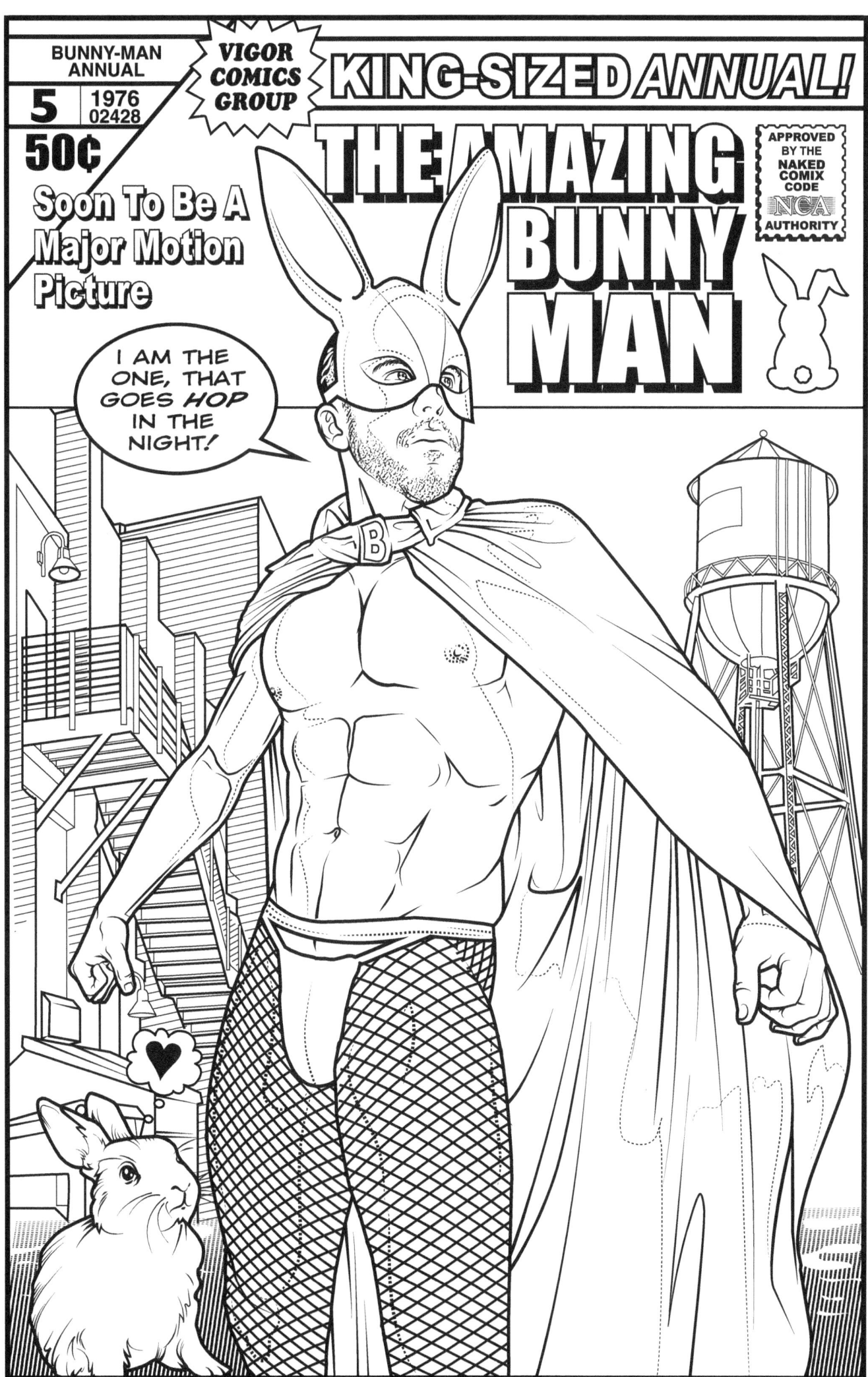

Bunny Bartender

Models: Leon G. Ray & Courtney Cass

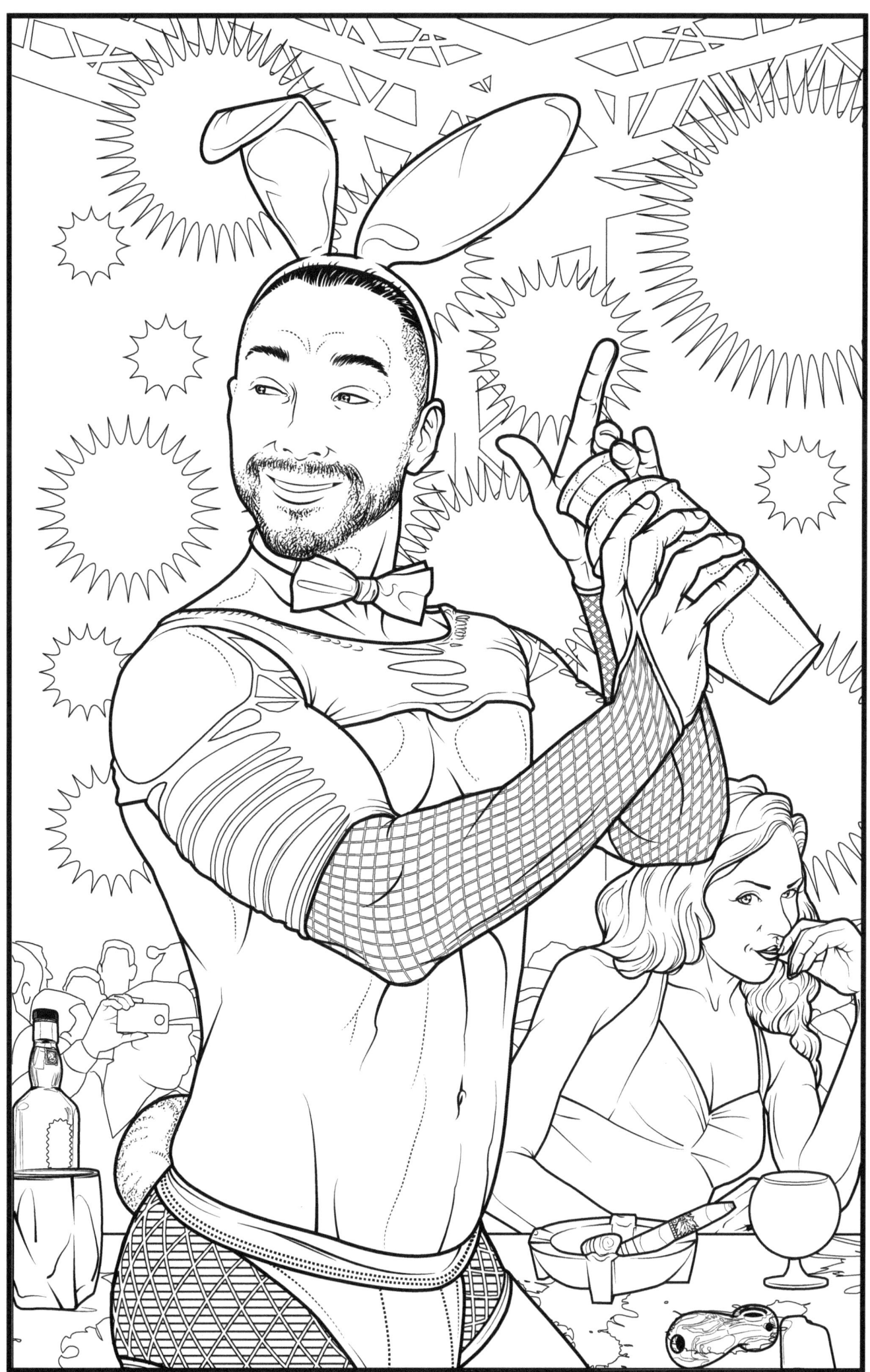

The Surrealist

Model: Lee Harvey Roswell

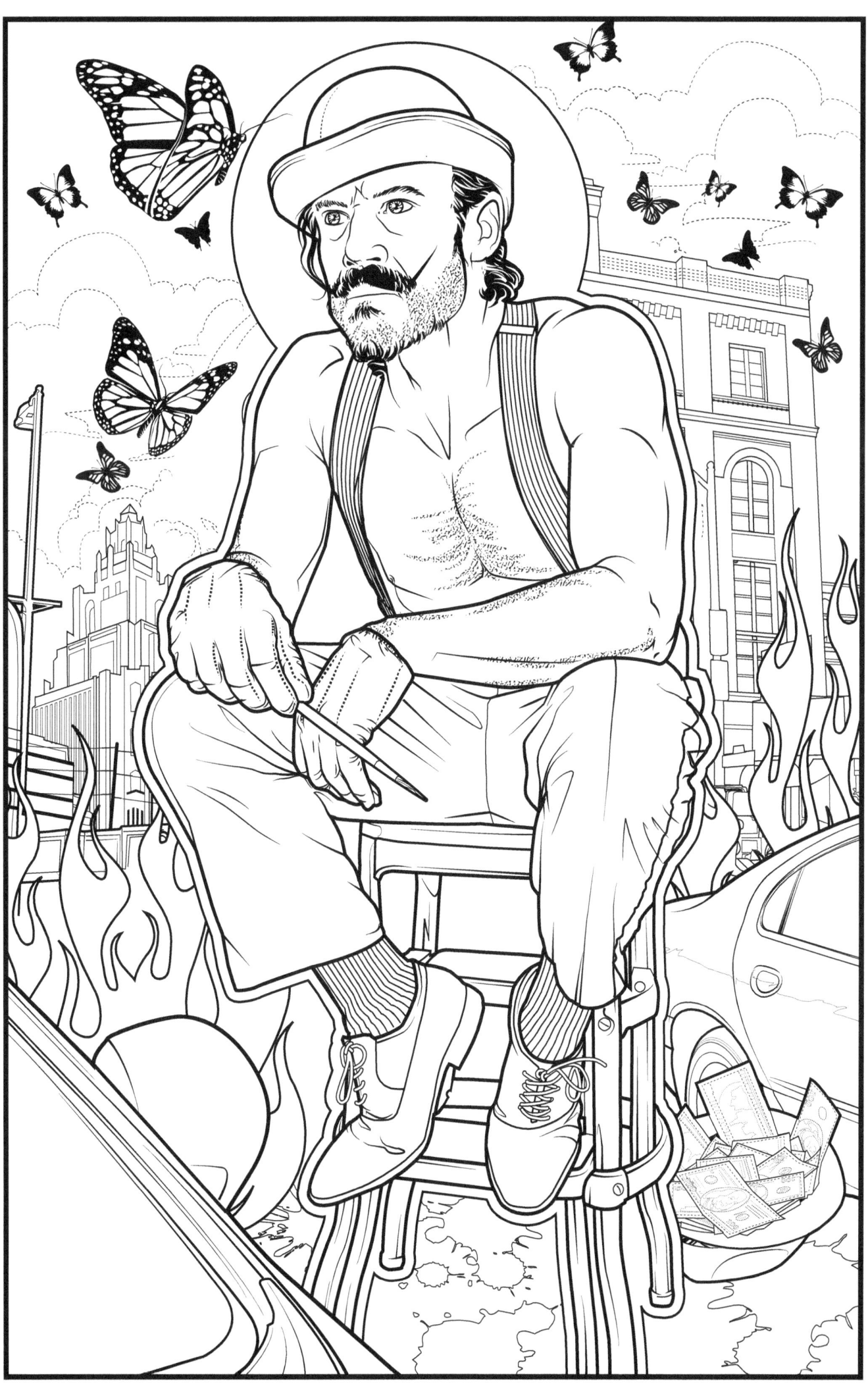

Evil Cupid

Model: Leon G. Ray

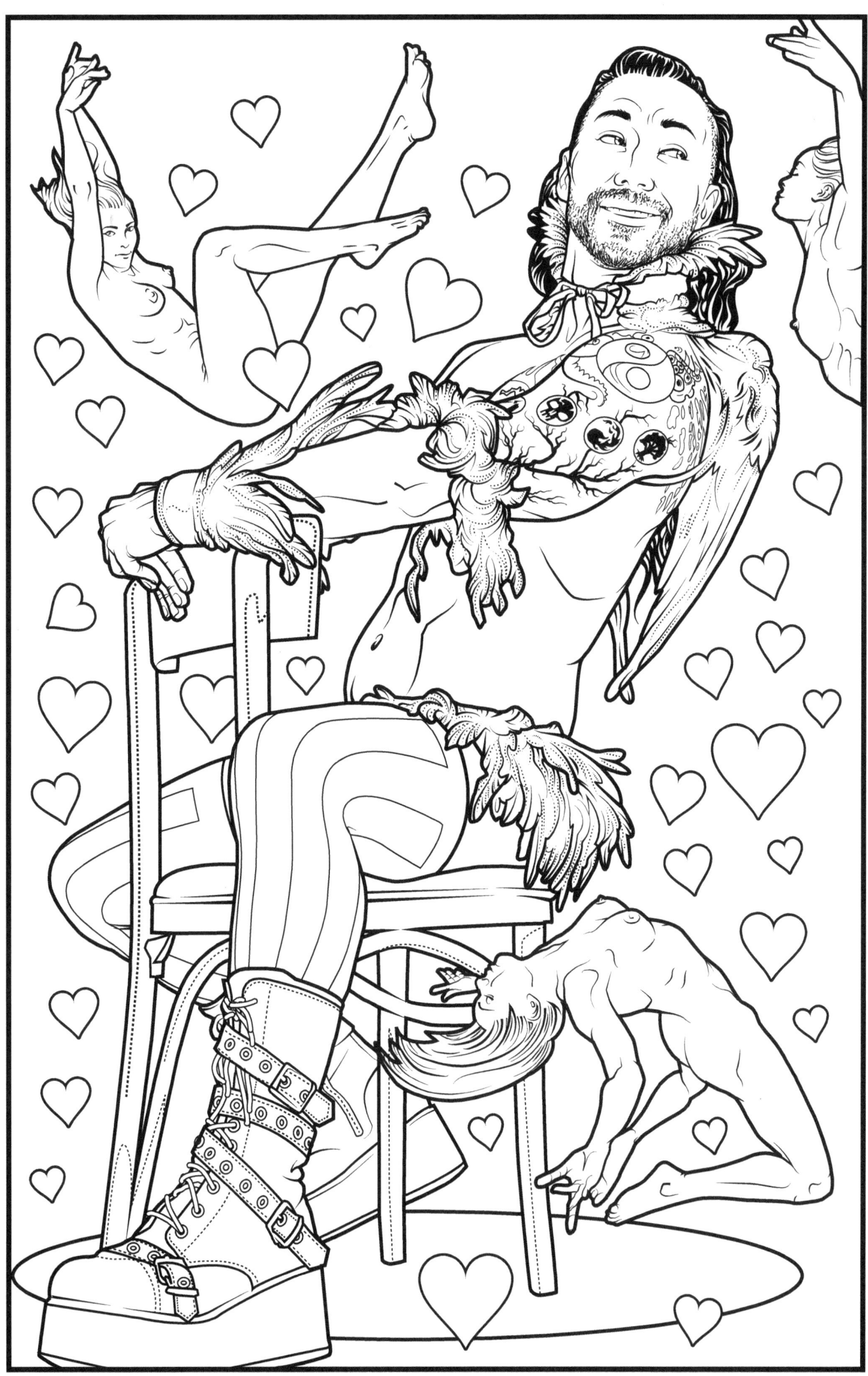

In The End...

Model: Ross Travis

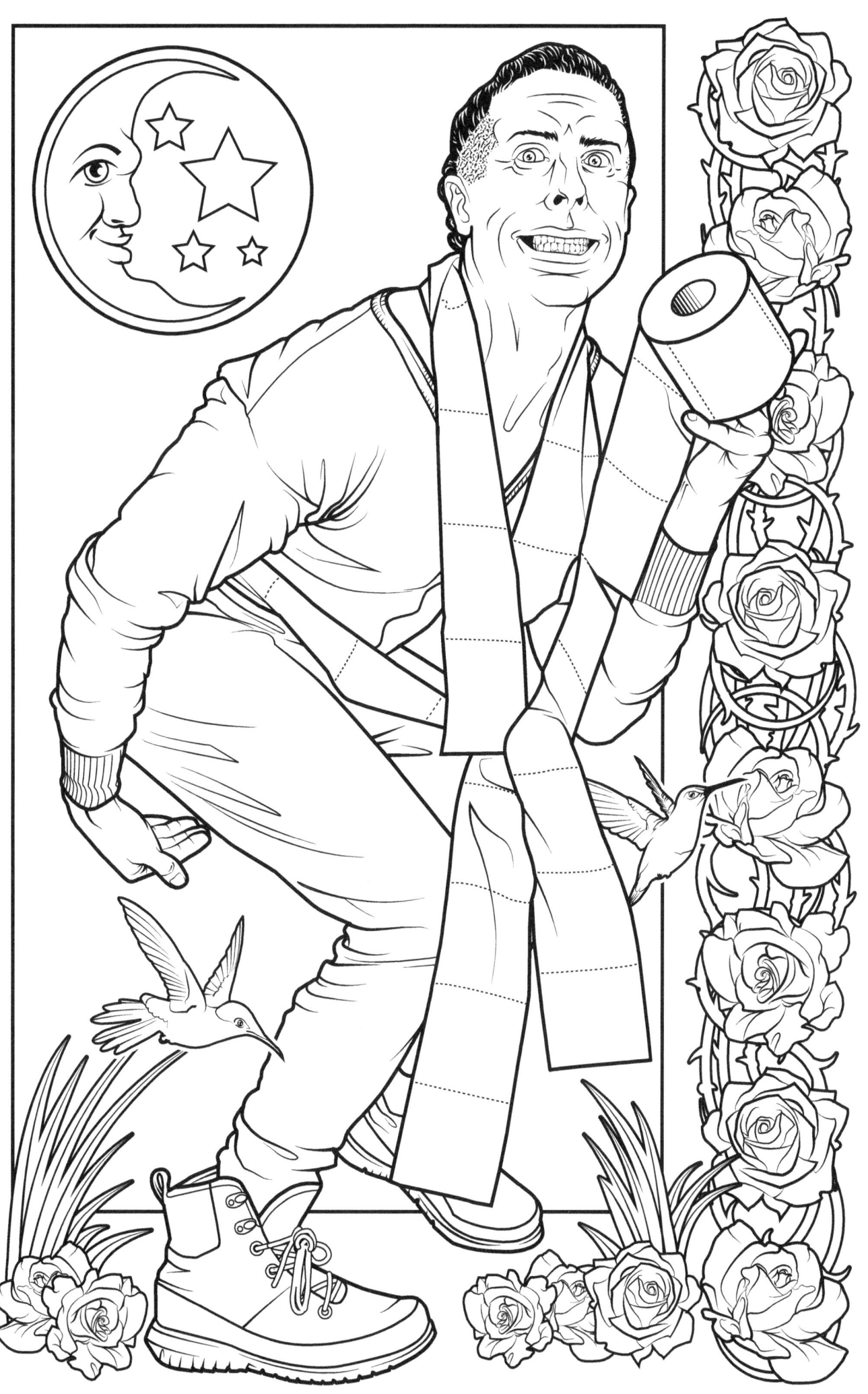

www.ingramcontent.com/pod-product-compliance
Lightning Source LLC
Chambersburg PA
CBHW041104170526
45159CB00016B/3126